Jame

Bethany Doreen Robinson

"Life is not measured by the number of years but by the amount of sensitivity you experience."

This Book is for:

....

....

....

....

....

CONTENTS

Chapter 1:
The Young Buck

The log cabin birthplace of James Buchanan, like other well-preserved remnants of the era in the grove in the heart of the Mercersburg Academy campus, where it was transported more than a half century ago, still appears pretty typical. Given its location on the grounds of a boarding school, the cabin appears to be a place where Santa Claus might sit during the holiday season, or where a docent dressed in nineteenth-century garb might stoke a fire, roast something in a kettle above it, and tell stories of brave pioneers heading west from Philadelphia, which is about a hundred miles away.

Prior to the 1953 relocation, the cabin was located in Chambersburg, the Franklin County seat, and served as the home of the county Democratic Party. It became outdated due to its tiny size and inability to be easily adapted for better communication links. However, on April 23, 1791, it was more or less cutting-edge, with Elizabeth Speer Buchanan, twenty-four, giving birth there to the second of eleven children she had with James Buchanan, whom she had married three years and a week previously.

The cabin was located at the Stony Batter crossroads, some three miles west of Mercersburg, which was already a prosperous community not far north of the Maryland border—what was to become the famed Mason and Dixon Line—and not far from midway between Philadelphia and Pittsburgh. The elder Buchanan had arrived in Pennsylvania in 1783 from County Donegal, where he was born in 1761, to make his fortune, much like previous and subsequent immigrants in what had just recently become the United States. Elizabeth Speer, the twenty-one-year-old daughter of a Scotch-Irish merchant who resided near Buchanan's uncle, a tavern keeper in York, close down the road toward Baltimore, was chosen as his wife. Buchanan chose a position on the trail west, near the small hamlet of Cove Gap, in a place called Stony Batter, and established a trade establishment, what would later be called a general store. He had first worked for a man named John Tom there, but eventually opened his own store further into the gap, where the route was bad and anyone trying to journey from Baltimore or Philadelphia to Pittsburgh that way needed to buy a lot of supplies.

According to one story, there were days when one hundred horse riders passed through Buchanan's Stony Batter store, which is significantly more than the daily visitors who go about a mile into the state park to see the obelisk marking the place where the younger Buchanan was born. There are few signs indicating it, and there isn't much parking for tourists. It is one of two memorials endowed by Harriet Lane, the younger Buchanan's favorite niece; the other is in Washington, DC, and was completed many years after the president died. The area around the Stony Batter monument is likely to have changed little since Buchanan was born there. Even in the twenty-first century, it appears like it would take an ambitious and hardworking individual to make a business succeed there.

But, before long, life grew a little easier for the Buchanans. James Senior first purchased a sizable property near Mercersburg, about four miles away and the largest town in the area with around one hundred residents, for £1,500. Then, in 1796, he chose to relocate to town, purchasing a two-story house on the main street, opening a store, and eventually becoming one of the area's wealthiest men.

Because the following five of James and Elizabeth Buchanan's children were daughters, James the younger was the second born (an elder sister having died as a newborn). The strain was plainly on from the boy's early boyhood, at least when the family arrived in the reasonably populated community of Mercersburg, that James would have to take the Buchanan family forward into the new American century.

What is known about Buchanan's childhood is primarily based on an undated memoir handed to George Ticknor Curtis by Buchanan's relatives. Buchanan attempted to enlist the help of friends to produce an official biography twice after leaving office, but each time it fell through. Several relatives and friends had retained Buchanan's numerous letters and jottings, and more than a decade after his death, they hired Curtis, who had written several historical works, to write a biography. Curtis claimed that he made it his duty to compose the book primarily from these materials, rather than other interviews or histories, and that it came to 644 pages and was published in 1883 by Harper & Brothers, a New York publishing business. Curtis stated that he does not apologize for rarely quoting others. Despite the fact that the family had not asked him to do so, he thought he had enough material from them to produce a respectable, if not entirely objective, biography.

There is no reason to suppose the otherwise unpublished memoir supplied to Curtis is anything other than Buchanan's work, as it reflects the often detached writing style typical of the many letters he penned during his professional life. According to later biographers, there are only a few phrases that describe his father, with whom he frequently disagreed, but those sentences commend him as a solid man.

"My father was a man of practical judgment, great industry, and perseverance," Buchanan said in his memoir. "He had a good English education and the kind of knowledge of mankind that kept him from being duped in his business."
"He was a man of great native force of character," Buchanan went on to say. "He was not only respected, but adored by everyone who met him... He was a loving father, a loyal friend, and a devout Christian."

Buchanan, on the other hand, was far more enthusiastic about his mother and her influence on him: "My mother was a remarkable woman, considering her limited opportunities in early life." She was the daughter of a country farmer, and although working in the family from childhood until my father's death, she found time to read a lot and think profoundly about what she read. She loved poetry and could easily recite any portion from one of her favorite authors that caught her attention.

Buchanan stated that his father had always hoped she would cease doing housework after he had made a lot of money, but she refused. Buchanan claimed that his mother was convinced that those chores were her destiny.

"She was a woman of great firmness of character and bore the afflictions of her later life with Christian philosophy," Buchanan wrote, regretting her loss even at the time. "Her influence was primarily responsible for her sons' liberal education." Under Providence, I dedicate any minor distinction I may have achieved in the world to the blessing He bestowed upon me by providing me with such a mother."

Buchanan, on the other hand, was not a mama's boy. Early on, he felt certain that he would be a successful adult no matter what path he took. Colleges had begun to sprout up in the outskirts. Most of the institutions founded in the eighteenth century were essentially male finishing schools for the elite: Harvard, Yale, Princeton, William and Mary, the University of Pennsylvania, and Queens College (later Rutgers). However, as the nineteenth century began, families of relative means, such as the Buchanans, came to believe that "college," whatever that truly meant in terms of additional education, was something they wanted for their sons.In the West, the South, and northern New England, universities such as the University of North Carolina, Muskingum University in Ohio, Davidson College, Oglethorpe University, Bowdoin College (which trained Franklin Pierce, Buchanan's predecessor), and others sprang founded.

Dickinson College became the school of choice for individuals in south-central Pennsylvania, and Buchanan's father persuaded him to go when he was sixteen years old and had completed his studies at Old Stone Academy in Mercersburg. Buchanan, on the other hand, believed Dickinson was a farce. Buchanan probably breezed through studies because his mother insisted on him reading the classics. At the time, "college" meant a three-year period of study, and Buchanan had already started as a junior, which was the word for the second year.

Buchanan was a bit of a wastrel at Dickinson—no, he was a major annoyance. He began his lifelong habit of smoking cigars there; in later years, he was known to chew the ends of unlit cigars, much like movie sharpies and gangsters did in the early days of cinema. Whatever she taught him about the classics, she never emphasized humility. At Dickinson, Buchanan saw himself as above reproach.

Everyone agreed that he was the sharpest kid, but the administration, at the very least, did not approve of his arrogance and disregard for school standards. Colleges, particularly those aspiring for success in the early nineteenth century, relied on nearly jackbooted allegiance and discipline. Dickinson lived on the edges of society, west of Mercersburg near Carlisle, just short of the Appalachian Mountains, which few explorers crossed. It needed a clean reputation, free of shenanigans (or even rumors of them), to attract the sons of the wealthy, or at least the money of those paying for them.

Dickinson, on the other hand, was going through a hard spell when Buchanan arrived. In fact, it was on the verge of bankruptcy. The school had been run out of its original building, which had been a grammar school prior to Dickinson's founding in 1783, so the founder, signer of the Declaration of Independence Benjamin Rush, commissioned the most prominent architect in Pennsylvania, Benjamin Latrobe, the designer of the US Capitol, to design a magnificent replacement building, New College, in 1803. Unfortunately, that winter, a wind-driven snow storm passed across the Cumberland Valley, reportedly scooping up some ashes from New College's basement and burning it down.

Buchanan, despite being sixteen and younger than many of his peers, was prepared for such a test on his first full time away from home. He didn't want to come across as a self-absorbed nebbish, and subsequently stated that "to be a sober, plodding, industrious youth was to incur the ridicule of the majority of the students."

"Without much natural tendency to become dissipated," Buchanan said, "and chiefly from the example of others, and in order to be considered a clever and spirited youth," he engaged in "every sort of extravagance and mischief." In his first year, 1808, he downed sixteen toasts at a Dickinson event, which was perhaps his crowning achievement in that sense.

Buchanan didn't worry about that aspect of his reputation because he had done well in school until one September Sunday morning when someone arrived at the door with a letter that his father opened and then tossed at him. Picking it up, he saw the writing of Dickinson's most sober professor, history and Latin teacher Robert Davidson, who had kicked Buchanan out of school for disruptive conduct. Davidson wrote to his father that James would have been expelled sooner, but his scholarship was so large that the trustees simply had to wait a little longer.

As we say in the twenty-first century, James freaked out. His father told him he had just one option: to beg Davidson and the board to stop his humiliating behavior, at least until he graduated the next year. He went straight to John King, the Presbyterian preacher in Mercersburg and Dickinson trustee who had suggested Buchanan go there. Buchanan promised to be calm and sober if King could persuade Davidson to reverse his dismissal. Davidson assumed Buchanan had been scared straight, so the board let him back in, and Buchanan dialed back his celebrations for the year.

However, when it came time to award accolades to the graduating class—the most important being a speaker at the graduation ceremony—Buchanan was passed over by the trustees, despite having the top marks in the class, for a kid who was a bit more quiet and respected by the professors personally. He vented his rage to his father, but the elderly man seemed unaffected. Buchanan's father advised him to accept his penalty and move on, but the bull head chose to compose a graduation speech instead. Meanwhile, a friend who had received the second honors—roughly equivalent to a salutatorian today—offered Buchanan his spot on the dais, a move that pleased neither the trustees nor Buchanan, who, arrogant as he was, stated that he would not accept a second-fiddle spot and demanded the first honor he believed he deserved.

Finally, on September 19, 1809, Buchanan was allowed to speak as an official non honoree. He delivered his oratory on "The Utility of Philosophy " in an open spot between his friend and the third student in line in academics. Buchanan never forgave Dickinson, later noting that he left Carlisle "feeling but little attachment towards the Alma Mater." He must have understood, though, that cleaning up his act while at Dickinson would serve him well in the next part of his life, law school in the sprawling town of Lancaster, the largest inland city in the United States, with a population of 6,000.

While Buchanan did frequent the taverns near his boarding house, he also decided that the two years he would spend with Hopkins would be spent studying the preceptor's courtroom and business style, as well as the law itself. Buchanan took satisfaction in being a strict constructionist when it came to law, which he attributed to his early studies at Dickinson and Lancaster.

Buchanan did not happen to be in Lancaster by chance. It was the commonwealth's capital at the time, and he had chosen that his career, while ostensibly in the law, would be in fact in politics. Lancaster had been the capital of the United States for only one day, on September 27, 1777, when Congress fled Philadelphia as the British advanced. The next day, Congress determined it was not far enough away from the British approach and proceeded west to York.

There was no better place to be in his field, the law, than either Philadelphia or New York. The courthouse at King and Queen Streets served as the hub for business, politics, civil disputes, and property law in the Commonwealth capital. People came from all around to get their concerns resolved, and they needed local lawyers to do so.

Buchanan agreed with his father's judgment of James Hopkins, particularly after seeing the home across the street from his boarding house. He was only eighteen when he arrived in London, but he saw a bright career ahead of him, and after three years of hard work and soliciting clients for his preceptor, he passed the bar in 1812. The brightest twenty-one-year-old lawyer in the commonwealth capital seemed to have a promising future.

But, just as he was about to step out and start rolling, the commonwealth legislature voted to shift the capital a couple of hours down the macadam to Harrisburg, the break point for river vessels arriving from the south and land-only freight going from the north along the strategically important Susquehanna River. This gave Harrisburg a better location for a commerce center, a meeting place for businesses who might benefit from a judicial and legislative system at that location. That seemed to be the trend for state capitals—Trenton on the Delaware, Richmond on the James, Hartford on the Connecticut, Providence inland near the bay and its islands, and Albany on the Hudson.

Buchanan considered it a personal insult. He had worked hard to lay the groundwork, and now these idiot lawmakers were fouling up a good system—for him, at least. He started with the guy who had been his least sympathetic ear—his father. He raced back to Mercersburg and, in his wailing about the capital's relocation, caught his father off guard for a brief time, possibly because the elder Buchanan still had seven children at home to worry about.

Young James was an arrogant type who sensed an opportunity. He assured his father that he could personally handle such difficulties, so he promptly obtained a horse and rode down to Kentucky against his father's desires. He explained to the elderly man that he was traveling to Kentucky for his health and that it would be a vacation. The father realized that was all nonsense, but after two months of trying to talk his son out of it, he gave up and prayed for the best.

When James arrived, though, it was not the hayseed territory he expected. It was near the capital at Elizabethtown, and when he arrived at the courts, all the local giants were there, including a man he would eventually clash with, Speaker of the United States House of Representatives Henry Clay, and all his political friends. Buchanan was out of his element—and under water in theirs.

"I went there with the intention of making a big impression—and who do you think I met?" Buchanan wrote later, with the benefit of hindsight enhancing his humility. "There stood Henry Clay! John Pope, John Allan, John Rowan, Felix Grundy—they were giants, sire, and I was a midget. The next day, I packed my trunk and returned to Lancaster—it was large enough for me. Kentucky was far too large."

When Buchanan returned to Lancaster, he approached his preceptor, Hopkins, and asked for a permanent position. Hopkins found him a better job—a government sinecure. The northern half of Lancaster County, which had been mostly rural but full with land speculators who wished to see it otherwise, was torn off and renamed Lebanon after its principal village.

The development provided an opportunity for Lancaster officials to dish out some favors, and Hopkins' close friend, Attorney General Jared Ingersoll, was in a position to do so. Lebanon County was going to need a young, energetic assistant prosecutor, and Hopkins, who didn't want the job, convinced Ingersoll to send it to his protégé Buchanan. It wasn't a full-time job, but it provided Buchanan with a base salary—perhaps $1,000 or $2,000 per year, enough to cover at least rent and board—and got him started on what seemed like an unexpected path, a political career.

He had largely studied property law under Hopkins. "I determined," he later wrote, "that if a severe application would make me a good lawyer, I should not fail in this particular... I studied law, and nothing but the law." After studying, he would take a break by walking out past downtown to the west, along Chestnut Hill, and look into the sunset—perhaps into the future—and go over in "speeches" what he had taught himself during the day. Buchanan was aware that the area around Lancaster was expanding, and while he was not particularly venal or mercenary, he desired to make a decent life through the law. Because public office did not appear to be the means to do this, he never expressed an interest in it.

It turned out to be a good thing, because his meticulous records reveal that he earned $938 in his first year of law practice in 1813, and an increase to $1,096 the next year. The typical technique for a young lawyer to get started—not dissimilar to those in solo practice in the twenty-first century—was to accept any unusual case an older lawyer would throw his way. They were frequently matters that were either too little or too inconvenient for an experienced lawyer, and no doubt Buchanan was content with whatever an established lawyer— either a mentor or a potential later connection—would hand off to him just to get started.

However, by 1814, the Lebanon County assistant prosecutor believed it was time to move on. Buchanan would come home every now and again and find himself discussing politics with his father. Both claimed to be Federalists, the party out of power, and complained about how the Madison government was bungling the "War of 1812" with Great Britain, which was already in its third year. At the moment, the best news at home was that his favorite sister, Jane, had married Elliot Lane, a man he liked. Despite the fact that he wrote nothing about it, he most likely returned to Mercersburg for the 1813 wedding ceremony.

Lancaster was a Federalist island in Pennsylvania's Democratic sea. Although George Washington was a nominal Federalist, John Adams was the party's only president. With the death of Alexander Hamilton, the party's rising star, in a duel with his Democratic rival Aaron Burr, enthusiasm for Federalist issues—primarily a strong federal bank and tariffs to finance desperately needed infrastructure projects in a growing nation—was dwindling. Young political leaders in Pennsylvania flocked to the Democrat-Republican Party of its heroes, Thomas Jefferson and James Madison, but Buchanan wanted to succeed in his chosen town, so he joined the local Federalists, as his father had done. Later in his career, when he became a Democrat, he justified his Federalist upbringing by claiming he was a product of his father's influence, an entirely excusable attribute when it came to the public, which was still predominantly affluent white men.

Buchanan joined the Washington Association, which was similar to today's Young Republicans and Young Democrats. He had risen to the presidency of the organization and delivered a passionate speech at a Fourth of July BBQ that was harshly critical of Madison's seeming mismanagement of the war effort. Still, he argued that Federalists should not be afraid to fight to change the path of the war.

Whether it was on purpose by Buchanan or by chance, the speech was well received by the senior Federalists in Lancaster. The British won a decisive battle at Bladensburg, outside the nation's capital, on August 24, and marched on Washington, burning public buildings, including the White House, with the Madisons barely escaping the blaze.

On August 25, a gathering for war volunteers was held in downtown Lancaster. As the new potential assemblyman, Buchanan delivered a speech and was the first to volunteer for whichever regiment was mounting itself out of Lancaster. Despite having no standing in the federal army or local or state militias, roughly two dozen young men from Lancaster, led by another lawyer, Henry Shippen, armed themselves with horses, pistols, long guns, and swords and rode off to Baltimore as the Lancaster County Dragoons.

As a torrent of rain descended on Buchanan and his fellow prospective horse thieves, they pitched their tents for the night, drenching Buchanan, who drew the traditional short straw and received the bunk close to the leaky tent wall. The next day, they gathered the necessary horses, no doubt infuriating the people of Ellicott Mills, and began marching them back to Baltimore. As they paraded down Market Street, the Lancaster volunteers who had managed to avoid embarking on the secret mission met them with loud laughter, causing the "heroes" to lose some of their zeal. By early September, following the famous British bombing of Fort McHenry, which inspired observer Francis Scott Key—a young lawyer like Buchanan—to write "The Star-Spangled Banner," the British had left Baltimore and the Lancaster County Dragoons had returned home, their dreams of war heroism dashed but all their limbs intact.

His military duty was, maybe fortunately, brief, and Buchanan easily won his first genuine election, but there came the predictable note from his father, who saw the dark while all around him was bright: "I hope you will make the best of the situation now," wrote the elder Buchanan. "I'm afraid of this taking you away from the bar at a time when you might need it the most."

Nonetheless, Buchanan set out for Harrisburg for the three-month legislative session with his customary youthful optimism. When he arrived, he discovered that the Pennsylvania Assembly was not the glorious assembly he had imagined. There were a number of local petitions, and because the commonwealth's courts were so sluggish and overburdened with cases, many of those petitions asked for private bills, their constituents feeling they had a better chance of getting personal legislation than a victorious or speedy court battle.

Buchanan, on the other hand, desired to see through the muck. He rapidly realized that the men who delivered speeches were the ones who were noticed, not the grinds who got those petitions pushed to the floor. There were individuals who could talk on the spur of the moment, but Buchanan was determined to prepare his remarks and leave nothing to chance. He opted to be a little controversial right away.

Even though the War of 1812 was nearly done, Philadelphia was still concerned about another British attack. The United States Congress had rejected a bill calling for universal conscription, but the Pennsylvania Senate felt that the federal government could not adequately defend the city's port and approved its own conscription legislation. The plan was for all men over the age of twenty-one to be separated into groups of twenty-two. One of those men would be drafted, and the other twenty-one would chip in to cover the cost of a $200 "bounty purse" for the unlucky conscript.

On February 1, 1815, Buchanan spoke out against the measure, proposing that the militia from the commonwealth be fully volunteer. It appeared that the British had no intention of extending the war anyway—in fact, peace came two weeks later—and putting up such effort to defend Philadelphia should not be on the commonwealth's agenda.

Despite his best efforts, the speech proved to be an auspicious introduction to the greater world of politics for young Buchanan, with ramifications for the remainder of his political career. Buchanan wanted to make the Federalist position on the war clear, therefore he focused solely on this bill.

When it came down to reality and discussion, the speech was like throwing a stone into a lake, with waves radiating out farther and farther. This rookie assembly member had taken on Philadelphia, the true seat of power in the commonwealth. That meant he was firmly putting the interests of the commonwealth's western section ahead of the rich and powerful eastern section. Furthermore, he was totally in favor of the poor over the rich—a poor man could not pay the "bounty purse" and would have to be one of the twenty-two to serve.

It's difficult to believe Buchanan's speech was intended to be so populist, but it set him apart from most Federalists, who, while opposing the war, would prefer to see men pay a fee if they didn't want to serve and, further, would want Philadelphia defended, as it was not only the seat of the Bank of the United States, but also one of the two largest merchant centers in the new country, along with New York.

According to Buchanan's own private papers, which were given to his authorized biographer George T. Curtis, the Democratic state senator from Mifflin County, William Beale, saw the speech as so far from the usual Federalist stance that he suggested Buchanan join his party immediately, thus not having to change his principles and views one bit.

Buchanan, who had expected to make at least a splash of grandeur, was devastated. He was not present in the legislature when the bill was put to a vote. Fortunately, when peace was established with England a few weeks later, the matter died. That was Buchanan's only speech of the term, and he even doubted himself, which was unusual for him, and decided not to run again. His father, true to his contradictory nature, advised him to forget the speech and its consequences and re-register for the assembly. This time, his father was more optimistic, claiming that another term would improve his chances of being elected to the US House of Representatives. He would always face opposition, but the best course of action was to regroup, recharge, and continue on.

Buchanan was pleased at his father's unexpected compliment. He returned to the Fourth of July gathering for the Lancaster Washington Association, held in front of the courthouse, to kick off his fresh campaign for the assembly. Buchanan lived in that area. His boarding house was just down the street, and his office was right around the corner from the large public square where the courthouse stood. He and Lancaster's prothonotary, John Passmore, a four-hundred-pound-man, had bought the building where they both had offices and apartments, not to mention a tiny pub downstairs, for $4,000 in cash the year before, with a $1,000 mortgage. Most likely, his father paid him in advance, just as a modern father would.

This was intended to be his official debut. This time, Buchanan was well prepared. He expected to be preaching to the converted. He was confident that this would be a friendly audience, a local boisterous crowd.

Portraits of Buchanan in his later years show him as a stuffy guy with starched collars and dour expressions, never a smile or a looseness about him. That is most likely a sign of the times, with painted portraits being formal and pictures requiring a lengthy time to make, necessitating the individuals sitting immobile. There are no paintings of Abraham Lincoln giggling, or of Robert E. Lee or Ulysses S. Grant riding sidesaddle with a twisted hat. The stiffer Buchanan of later life contradicts all physical descriptions of him as a young man.

Buchanan was described as having distinctive appearance, with blue eyes, wavy blond hair, and strong shoulders. He had a condition that prevented him from growing body or face hair. That would not have served him well in the era of the bearded presidents of the late nineteenth century (Lincoln, Grant, Garfield, Hayes, and Benjamin Harrison), but clean-shaven ness was the norm. He walked quickly and spoke in a sonorous, deep voice. He was at least six feet tall, which was not quite a giant in those days, but just above-average for a strong man.

Aside from his absence of body and facial hair, he possessed one more peculiar physical feature. He was nearsighted in one eye and farsighted in the other, and his pupils wandered occasionally when he tried to stare. As a result, he frequently bent his head when speaking to people, merely to obtain a better view of them, giving the impression that he was so interested in them that he needed to come closer. His second biographer, Philip Klein, who honestly believed Buchanan's reputation had been tainted over the years, described this physical gesture as "a perpetual attitude of courteous deference and attentive interest." Many people mistakenly believed that they had completely captivated James Buchanan and were reciprocated by attention to him that he attributed to traits more complimentary to him than a wry neck upon first meeting him. Buchanan made an excellent 'first impression' on practically everyone he met, thanks in part to this physical oddity."

As he prepared to appear on July 4, 1815, Buchanan's reputation was firm. His legal knowledge was his greatest asset as a lawyer. He did not demonstrate his intelligence, but rather his tenacity. He was well-prepared while others were haphazard, and tireless when others slacked. He was also the personification of the "hale fellow, well met" in social occasions. He was never too front or too far back in the crowd. He enjoyed cigars, the darker the better, and drank perhaps a little more than he should have, but only a little, especially Madeira, the wine of the colonies and hence ideal for a Federalist.

In both word and spirit, he delivered the speech he had intended. He was not thinking about changing to Democrat-Republicanism, as Senator Beale of Mifflin County had scolded, and his words could have been those of any presidential candidate in a primary contest in the present era. It was full of venom, half-truths, and blatant partiality. He referred to his opponents as "demagogues" and "functionaries," "friends of the French" troubled by "diabolic passions." He even argued that the Democrats did not believe in the Constitution because their party was called the "anti-Federalists."

He said that the Democrats were the party of anarchy. When they assumed power in 1800, they abolished the navy, leaving merchant ships unsafe, and they went farther to cut out commerce by insisting on embargos. They attacked the Federal Reserve Bank of the United States, further hampering company creation, and halted the national tax that funded the new country's infrastructure.

As the metaphorical final nail in the coffin, Buchanan said, they declared war, a war they couldn't afford. Instead of being carried close to the breast by our natural allies, the English were the bad guys, and the Democrats surrendered to the wastrel French.

Napoleon Bonaparte was the Democratic Party's nominal head, and James Madison served to benefit personally from the relationship.

The speech was a success in local politics, with the Washington Association printing copies and distributing them throughout the commonwealth. Buchanan received renomination and reelection, but also the wrath of Jeffersonians, notably Democrats in Lancaster County and adjacent.

His father, once again, adopted the opposing viewpoint. He admitted to his son that he was too harsh in his criticism of the Democrats. His father reminded Buchanan that he had friends in the opposing party, and that Lancaster was too tiny to allow those friendships to fade.

It might not have mattered this time because he was going to be elected as a Federalist. But the power of that party was eroding. Buchanan would be ready for that, but his speech and the reputation he established that day would come back to haunt him later, since Democrats in the commonwealth have long, long memories.

In any case, his assembly career ended the following year. The Lancaster Federalists had a tradition of serving no more than two terms before handing over his seat to someone else, in this case his buddy Jasper Slaymaker. Buchanan had been as frustrated with the Federalists as he had with the Democrats. The former seemed to always want to safeguard the rights of the wealthy, while the latter seemed to always want to incite the rabble. He needed time away from politics for this reason, as well as time to dedicate to law work, as his working capital was still quite low.

Buchanan began working on his law profession, becoming a general practitioner as much as anything else. His reputation remained the same as when he was a young apprentice—he diligently researched every subject and always arrived at court well prepared. He wasn't flamboyant, but when he had a chance, he generally won. As luck would have it, he eventually got a case that catapulted him to stardom.

With the war against Great Britain still raging, the Pennsylvania militia was merged into the federal army, but a young Lancaster man named Houston elected not to fight in July 1814. He was court-martialed by the Pennsylvania militia and convicted, but he appealed to Franklin's court, and the Federalist judge held that because the Pennsylvania militia had been part of the federal military at that time, it had no right to trial young Houston.

The case was taken all the way to the United States Supreme Court, which overturned the verdict, and Franklin was impeached in 1816 by the state legislature, which had overwhelmingly turned Democrat by that point.

Franklin chose Buchanan as his lawyer because he believed he could win his case. Even in those days, it would have been rare for a judge to entrust his reputation to a twenty-five-year-old lawyer, but there were at least three probable explanations, according to Buchanan's advocate biographer, Philip Klein. The simplest explanation is that the two were clearly buddies because they were downtown Lancaster neighbors and fellow Federalists. When he was in the Pennsylvania Assembly, Buchanan was alarmed by Democratic witch hunts of judges. Buchanan claimed to be a rigorous constructionist of the Constitution throughout his life. He made mistakes later in his career, particularly as president, but he clearly saw the separation of the three branches of government being cruelly broken by the legislature. Finally, Buchanan had just recently departed the assembly, and Franklin was aware that Buchanan was widely respected by members of both parties.

In his defense of Judge Franklin, Buchanan adhered to the separation of powers doctrine and did not personally indict anyone. He pointed out that the action against Judge Franklin was initiated primarily because the Democrats did not agree with his judgment, not because he was negligent in making it. His reasonably neutral argument was a popular winner. The impeachment managers had the trial adjourned for several weeks before returning and presenting a weak prosecution, forcing the state senate to acquit Franklin.

Nonetheless, there was a target on Franklin's judicial robes. The Pennsylvania Assembly impeached Judge Franklin again in February 1817, this time because he declared that two Lancaster lawyers may keep a $300 judgment they had secured for a plaintiff since they were entitled that amount as legal fees. After the lower house voted two to one against Franklin, Buchanan enlisted the help of an old mentor, James Hopkins, and together they convinced the state senate to acquit him.

It didn't take long for the legislature to attack Judge Franklin once more, this time seeking an impeachment based on a ruling rather than Franklin's character or wrongdoing. This time, Buchanan was truly blessed. The assembly and the senate quarreled over who had precedence over which chamber would hear the impeachment. It became so raucous that assembly members invaded the senate chambers, some even climbing through the windows, to disrupt senate activity or simply to shout at one another.

When things cooled down a few weeks later, the impeachment process began, but Judge Franklin had become a minor actor by that point, and the legislators were more concerned with their own infighting. Buchanan easily earned Judge Franklin's third acquittal.

While the publicity surrounding the three impeachments certainly enhanced Buchanan's legal reputation, Judge Franklin's fees ensured that he was financially secure. In 1815, Buchanan earned a respectable $2,000. It had doubled to $8,000 by 1818, the year of the last trial. This elevated him to the pantheon of the Lancaster legal world, establishing him as an aesthetic and financial success while still in his twenties.

Buchanan had gone far beyond what his father could have anticipated. His mother may have intended him to be a priest, but as much as he admired her, he was content with his choice of law. He was ready to take the next step, whatever it was, and it may take him further away from Lancaster than his current observers imagined.

Buchanan would often end the day in one of the downtown Lancaster taverns when he was in the assembly or soon after. He felt most at ease with individuals of his profession who were his age, as would any young professional today. He admired those whose station was slightly higher than his, such as his first Lancaster friend, Jasper Slaymaker, whose family had become wealthy through business and speculation, and Amos Ellmaker, who had attended prestigious Yale University in Connecticut before coming to study with Buchanan at James Hopkins.

Molton C. Rogers, the son of Delaware's governor, was one of Ellmaker's friends from Litchfield, a town near Yale where he had first studied law. Rogers, like Slaymaker, "was born with a silver spoon in his mouth and was already tied to the high society crowds of Lancaster and Philadelphia," according to Patrick Clarke, the director of Wheatland, Buchanan's last home in Lancaster.

In 1816, Buchanan decided to form a sort of collaboration with Rogers, not necessarily because of this. They had become close after eating at the same "bachelor mess," a loosely organized men's dining club, and found their perspectives on life to be similar, although coming from different backgrounds. Rogers was from money and tone, but Buchanan was not, according to Clarke. Buchanan was of mountain descent. His father was successful to some extent. He was not as affluent as Rogers and his friends. He had eleven children, which meant he had a lot of mouths to feed. He made a decent living, yet he was a grocer."

Rogers and his supporters were delighted to welcome Buchanan. Rogers relocated his practice to Buchanan's East King Street building, gaining acceptance into Lancaster society, such as it was. Buchanan was one of the organizers of the yearly Lancaster society ball by October. The following month, Rogers and John Reynolds, a Farmers Bank officer, sponsored him for the Masonic lodge, into which he was initiated in December. The Masons, a rather mysterious group, had an important role in politics and business dealings. George Washington, like many of the Founding Fathers and presidents throughout the centuries, was a Mason. Buchanan stayed with the organization for a long time, eventually rising to the position of deputy grand master in his region.

Soon, Buchanan's social scene shifted from pub back rooms to the parlors of the fashionable and wealthy in Lancaster and, on occasion, Philadelphia. His wages rose, and his clever maneuverings for a respected judge made him a sought-after invitee. There is little doubt that he was regarded as Lancaster's most eligible bachelor, and many of his invitations were no doubt intended to introduce him to families' marriageable daughters.

Rogers began courting Eliza Jacobs, the daughter of Cyrus Jacobs, who made his money from iron works, about a year after the two men formed their business relationship. Eliza's brother was a pupil of Buchanan, who had become one of the town's go-to lawyers for apprentices. Rogers proposed that Buchanan accompany Eliza's cousin, Ann Caroline Coleman, to a party one day, and Buchanan agreed without hesitation.

The grocer's son had just won the huge prize. Ann Coleman's father, Robert, was one of the wealthiest men in America. He, like Buchanan's father, moved from Ireland in the mid-eighteenth century, working as a worker and clerk for an ironmaster in Reading, a few miles north of Lancaster, and marrying the master's daughter. Coleman had a half-dozen iron firms by the time John Adams became president, making him one of the young country's first self-made millionaires.

By all accounts, he was obsessed with his daughter. She was described as beautiful and mercurial, sometimes demure and wild. She was twenty-two years old when she met Buchanan, who was living as an unmarried lady at the time. Robert Coleman, who had come from nothing, was not going to allow his daughter to marry a bad match. His oldest daughter had married Judge Joseph Hemphill of Philadelphia, who had previously served in Congress before his judicial position. Coleman, at seventy-one, was unsure he was the correct choice when Ann became serious about Buchanan.

Buchanan seemed to have his reservations as well, not so much about Ann as about whether he was destined for the then-newly wealthy. The wealthy in America were still striving to figure out who they were. This was no England, Spain, or France, with barons and earls, centuries-old fortunes, and strict regulations governing who might even come into contact with whom. It wasn't like Buchanan had to slay a dragon or find some royal blood to move up in society, but he wasn't sure he was comfortable being treated so well when he went to someone's mansion party and not having the resources to pay back. Because the Coleman family's influence was so pervasive in eastern Pennsylvania, the invites sometimes lasted days, with feasts and parties happening all the time. Buchanan loved it for the time being, but he realized that if he married Ann Coleman, he'd have to be the instigator, not simply the recipient, of some of these galas.

Nonetheless, Buchanan proposed to Ann in the summer of 1819, just as his friend Molton Rogers married Eliza Jacobs. Lancaster was buzzing with the news of both potential unions. Will there be two weddings? Would one family try to outdo the other? Would one of the young lawyers give up the law and work in the iron industry instead? The Colemans, on the other hand, were said to be skeptical of their possible son-in-law. Coleman served as a trustee at Dickinson College and was well aware of Buchanan's unsavory reputation there. He may not have appreciated the antics of Buchanan and his young pals in Lancaster, who drank a lot, relished in practical jokes, and frequently squandered their money foolishly.

Nonetheless, Buchanan persisted in his courtship. However, the country experienced a financial panic in late 1819. Buchanan, who had returned to being a property lawyer, was swamped with employment as land was quickly acquired and sold, while bankruptcy and foreclosure cases clogged the courtrooms. Buchanan was involved with Farmers Bank and a buddy there, William Jenkins. He was constantly traveling to Philadelphia, which hampered his betrothed's partying in Lancaster.

His political situation was also in disarray, since the Federalist Party's popularity was decreasing. For the first time, Buchanan joined a party committee with Jenkins and his preceptor, James Hopkins, to try to persuade the commonwealth's members of Congress to vote against the proposed Missouri Compromise, which would allow Maine to secede from Massachusetts and become a free state while allowing Missouri to enter the Union as a slave state. This was Buchanan's first public stance against slavery, and indeed his first stance on any nationally contentious issue.

Then there was the devastating event, which might now make its way to the public via BuzzFeed, TMZ, or Entertainment Tonight. Buchanan went by to see the Jenkins family on his way home from out of town at the end of November. He ran upon Mrs. Jenkins's sister, Grace Hubley, who was visiting. Needless to say, Grace was graceful and beautiful; had she been old and decrepit, perhaps the fate of America would have changed dramatically forty years later.

Instead, someone told Ann Coleman about Buchanan's supposed eyeing of Grace Hubley, and she became enraged since Buchanan would have stopped anyplace before meeting her, but surely not somewhere such as Grace Hubley would be. Ann promptly broke off the engagement in a letter, which was allegedly given to Buchanan at the courthouse, where he was stated to turn pale. His emotions shattered, he did nothing right away.

Ann, on the other hand, appeared to be angry and chose to accompany her younger sister, Sarah, to meet their elder sister, Margaret, who had relocated to Philadelphia, at the request of her mother. They left Lancaster on December 4, but she got sick on the way to Philadelphia, where she had planned to watch some plays and operas. She apparently did not, spending much of her time at her sister's house resting.

Two days later, Buchanan received a settlement in a major dispute, preserving the Columbia Bridge Company, in which several of his friends had a stake. This was on a Monday, and Buchanan apparently had work to do for the rest of the week, but he may have felt he could make amends with Ann by the weekend.

That, however, was not to be. Thursday morning, Buchanan learned the devastating news that had gripped Lancaster and Philadelphia: Ann Coleman had died. In his diary, Judge Thomas Kittera, a friend of the Colemans and afterwards of Buchanan, wrote:

I encountered this young lady on the street at midday yesterday [December 8], in the strength of heath, and only a few hours later[,] her friends were lamenting her death. She had been engaged to be married, but due to an unfortunate misunderstanding, the marriage was called off. This situation was weighing heavily on her mind. In the day, she was suffering from hysteria; in the evening, she was so well that her sister took her to the theater. After nightfall, she was assaulted with intense hysterical convulsions, prompting the family to summon doctors, who expected this to pass quickly, as it did; however, her pulse gradually decreased till she died at midnight. Dr. Chapman says it's the first time he's heard of hysteria causing death. What horrible intelligence—what a lesson of wisdom does it convey to beloved parents sixty miles away—to a younger sister whose evening was spent in mirth and folly. Beloved and admired by everybody who knew her, in her prime, with all the advantages of education, beauty, and fortune, she was cut off in an instant.

There was no evidence of Ann Coleman committing suicide because there was no public autopsy, yet Judge Kittera's statement that her doctor had never encountered a case of hysteria causing death raises the possibility that she did. In any case, whatever the clinical grounds of Ann's death, many blamed it on Buchanan and his apparent neglect of his feelings.

It is obvious that the Colemans felt this way. "There is now no time for explanation," Buchanan wrote, "but the time will come when you will discover that she, as well as I, have been much abused." God forgive the perpetrators... I may be able to deal with the sorrow of her passing, but I believe that happiness has left me forever." The Colemans apparently never saw those remarks because they declined the note when it was delivered by a messenger and returned it unopened. Buchanan requested to see her body and accompany her casket as a mourner, but the Colemans refused. He stayed with his former client, Judge Franklin, who lived next door to the Colemans, but even the judge couldn't shake the Colemans' contempt for Buchanan. Buchanan attempted to write a memorial to Ann for publication in the local paper, but was overtaken by sadness, and Judge Franklin produced a very mundane one for him.

Buchanan rested for the rest of December. He went to his house in Mercersburg and, most likely, took a short holiday from work, as the courts are closed for Christmas and New Year's. He may have been in sadness, regrouping, or rage because the Colemans were so cold to him.

Even then, he must have understood that this would be a watershed moment in his life. He'd have to heal from Ann's death as well as the rumors about him that circulated around Lancaster and Philadelphia. Strangely, Ann Coleman's death may have led him onto a road he would not have taken otherwise.

Chapter 2:
The Man Who Wants to Be President Over and Over Again

Buchanan returned to Lancaster a man full of himself after his stint in Russia. In a passive-aggressive gesture, he purchased the Coleman house on East King Street, where his late fiancée had grown up and where he courted her. It was a large house for a single man, yet it was his, as though in place of his purported love.

But how long would he stay? He saw himself barred from running for the US Senate seat up for election in 1833, either because of the time of his return from Russia or because of internal state Democratic politics. And he'd grown tired of the regular cases he'd take on as a lawyer in Lancaster.

He began to consider alternative possibilities.
The Democratic faction based in Philadelphia, led by George Dallas, who would eventually become James Knox Polk's vice president, would make it difficult for Buchanan to establish himself as a legal force in the commonwealth's capital, so he considered seeking legal employment in New York or Baltimore.

He did, however, make one trip to Washington to see President Jackson. There were two major political crises that had arisen while he was in Russia. The first was Jackson's veto of a bill rechartering the United States Bank. Jackson despised the idea of a central bank, believing it would limit the nation's expansion and, in any case, be managed by opponents, and Jackson saw himself as a benign dictator, brighter than the average man and desiring to maintain power, at least in politics.

The other issue was one that Buchanan struggled with. It was South Carolina's repeal of the tariff agreements of 1828 and 1832 that was so crucial to Buchanan's pact with the Czar. Buchanan had long considered whether a state could overturn a federal statute and what would happen if it chose to exit the Union instead. His strict constructionist view of the Constitution did not specify a solution.

But he was a Unionist, and when Jackson threatened military action to force South Carolina to accept the tariffs, and the state bowed, Buchanan was relieved.

He also recognized that in order to get Jackson's favor, he would have to be both anti-Bank and anti-nullification. The latter was simple, but as a former Federalist and supporter of a centralized economy in general, he attempted to find a middle path on the bank problem. He revealed to Jackson that he had old Federalist beliefs, but said that because he believed in the general, he would not say anything about a central bank. Dallas and his Philadelphia friends were pro-Bank because the bank had been in Philadelphia for a long time and was crucial to the local economy. Because of this, Jackson was cool with them.

Jackson himself was trapped. He never liked Buchanan, but he despised the party's Bank-loving Philadelphia group much more, because they stood in the way of something essential to him: the destruction of the Bank of the United States. Jackson had it in for William Wilkins since he had voted in favor of rechartering the Bank in the Senate. Buchanan may have returned from his Siberian exile as a hero, but the circumstances were now such that it would not happen again, with the mercantile contract completed. So Wilkins left for the St. Petersburg mission, providing an opening for Jackson and his anointed successor, Martin Van Buren, to reward Buchanan a little. Instead of seeking a law firm in New York or Baltimore, Buchanan was returning to Washington to finish the two years left on Wilkins' United States Senate seat.

Buchanan was finally back on the road he had intended to be on. Although Van Buren was the next in line, Buchanan was just forty-three years old. He could pause for a moment, then proceed in his usual slow and measured manner. Even his defender, Philip Klein, stated in President James Buchanan: "James Buchanan always did things the slow way, the hard way, the sure way." He lacked the ability to make a surprise deadly move, a beautiful stroke, a bold risk, or a fast joke that sidestepped a situation in a fit of laughing. He made no attempt to modify his own attitude or to offer the Pennsylvania Democracy fresh meaning or direction. He began laboriously rebuilding his influence from the ground up, beginning with Lancaster County."

Meanwhile, Pennsylvania appeared to be moving Whig, which would undoubtedly hurt Buchanan's chances of reelection to the Senate in 1836, but Buchanan, always looking forward, may have known that something would blow his way. This time, it was the hubris of Lancaster's second political titan, the noisy and self-assured Thaddeus Stevens, who had likewise moved to Lancaster as a lawyer and was a member of the Commonwealth Assembly by 1835.

The Whigs and Anti-Masonic Party held 76 of the 100 seats in the Pennsylvania Assembly, with the Democrats failing due to the Jackson-induced schism in banking and tariff dealings. Stevens saw this as an opportunity to further tarnish the Democrats by linking them to the elitist, secretive, and feared Masonic movement. Stevens launched an investigation into the FreeMasons in December 1835, summoning every major Democrat to testify in Harrisburg. Because he was already in Washington, Buchanan was able to bypass this issue—he was, after all, a Mason. The entire plan backfired on Stevens and the Whigs. It was obvious what he was doing, and it was completely ineffective and nasty. It brought the Democrats back together and even enraged fellow Whigs, who distanced themselves from the Anti-Masons, hurting any coalition they may have had.

While Buchanan had done nothing significant in his first months in the Senate other than continuously advocating in support of anything Jackson supported, Stevens' overreach worked in his favor. Buchanan backed Van Buren in the 1836 presidential election and clung to his coattails tightly. Van Buren won by a scant 2,183 votes in Pennsylvania, and the Whigs were unable to field a viable opponent, thus there was only marginal resistance to Buchanan from some Bank-leaning Democrats.

Buchanan was now set—elected by his entire state, and thus the leader of his party in that state. For the first time, he had a long-term employment, six years in the Senate, perfect for a guy who "always did things the slow way, the hard way, the sure way."

When he arrived in Washington, he tracked down an old acquaintance, Senator William R. King of Alabama, and they agreed to share a room. Whatever their sexual relationship was, and there has been much speculation in the 180 years since, they were part of a cadre of Southern gentlemen and Northern Doughfaces, the nickname for Northern politicians who could be molded to Southern ideals, who admired them.

Most of the more notable Doughfaces, including eventual presidents Buchanan and Franklin Pierce, were not from significant social families and were therefore disliked by those in the North who were. When they arrived in Washington, they gravitated toward Southerners, who, whether affluent or poor, had different social graces that led them to accept nearly anyone into their social circles in the capital. Friendship may have trumped earlier political preferences. Before his Senate tenure, Buchanan had no history of supporting slavery, or even thinking or writing about it. King, on the other hand, owned many slaves on his farm in Selma, Alabama, and was most likely involved in the slave trade in his home North Carolina before it was prohibited. The majority of King's Washington acquaintances were Southerners, and they were the majority of Buchanan's social circle.

In reality, only a few years before, in 1834, Buchanan purchased the freedom of two slaves, a mother and daughter, from the Virginia-based family of his brother-in-law, Reverend Robert Henry, husband of his sister Harriet. Buchanan was making his political return from his Russian venture at the time, and he recognized that being perceived as a Northerner with slaves so close to him was unacceptable. He arranged for their liberation himself, and the daughter worked for him as a domestic servant—but a paid servant—for a time.

Around the same time in 1834, Buchanan made another seemingly insignificant decision, but one that would be significant in his personal life until his death. He recognized he would need someone to look after the old Coleman home he had purchased, as he expected some job to take him to Washington or beyond. The White Swan Hotel, directly on the courthouse square near his house, was one of his favorite restaurants. The proprietor's niece, who had just turned twenty-eight, had begun cooking and cleaning at the hotel, and Buchanan asked her if she would mind remaining at the house— whether he was there or not—and making sure it was clean and ready for him when he returned from Washington. Esther Parker, known as Miss Hetty, would remain his housekeeper and closest confidante for the next thirty-four years, maybe second only to his niece Harriet Lane, and probably the one to whom he whispered his dying words.

Those last remarks, though, would be a long time coming. Buchanan's star was rising. He was elected chair of the Senate Foreign Relations Committee, defeating the strong former Secretary of State Henry Clay, a Whig. When another of his Pennsylvania opponents, George Dallas, was appointed to that old exile post—the ministership in Russia—his position became even more secure. Buchanan did his regular plodding job, ensuring sure bills were paid and the president was informed of what Congress thought of his foreign policy, but his Senate life was devoid of excitement.

However, presidential politics were definitely on his mind. Van Buren was certain to run for a second term—every incumbent before him had, though John Adams and his son, John Quincy, had failed to win—but he was also likely to drop his running mate, Richard M. Johnson, whom he blamed for bringing the ticket down in 1836.

Buchanan struck a deal with King, his best friend and Senate president pro tempore. He would lobby for King to be the next vice presidential candidate, and if elected, King would state unequivocally that he would not run for president when Van Buren's anticipated second term expired in 1844, paving the door for a Buchanan campaign.

Buchanan's plan, as is his wont, was centered on whose "turn" it will be by that time. Van Buren was from New York, therefore the state has a long history. Johnson was born in Kentucky; Jackson was born in Tennessee; Calhoun, Jackson's first vice president, was born in South Carolina; Adams was born in Massachusetts; and the three presidents before him were born in Virginia. The Deep South would be well served by King's nomination. Pennsylvania, the second most populous state, had no one in the national executive office, not even a cabinet member.

To be sure, it would appear that it would be Buchanan's time in 1844.

Buchanan's plan never materialized. Van Buren remained faithful to Johnson despite the fact that the election was doomed from the start. In 1837, there was a downturn, which aided the Democratic campaign to demolish the Bank of the United States, which was regarded as a bulwark of economic stability by both the merchant and working classes. The Whigs gained traction in the off-year election of 1838, and then did a Jacksonian thing by supporting a military hero, William Henry Harrison, as their presidential candidate in 1840.

Not only did he fail to put his plan into action, but Buchanan also witnessed the Whigs' presidential ticket win Pennsylvania—albeit by only 350 votes out of 300,000—in the 1840 election, which was a landslide for Harrison, on whose coattails the Whigs carried both the House and Senate.

Buchanan may hope for the nomination, but the odds were long, and he hadn't had the normal time to devise a fresh plan. In some ways, it was astonishing that Buchanan could even consider running for president. He had spent nearly two decades as a lawmaker, either in the House or the Senate, by the time he was re-elected senator in 1842. His contemporaries included five future presidents (Van Buren, Tyler, Polk, Fillmore, and Pierce) as well as prominent luminaries ranging from Webster, Clay, Calhoun, and Benton to his friend King, Jefferson Davis, and, later, John Quincy Adams. He'd never had his name on any big legislation, given any prominent address, or even been anything more than a bystander in any key argument. His most celebrated achievement—getting the trade pact with Russia—was mostly owing to time, but even if he were given full credit, this was Russia, not Great Britain, France, Spain, or the Netherlands.

Despite this, Buchanan's name was frequently mentioned whenever positions of prominence were on the table, if not at the time, then in the future. Looking back, it appears that Buchanan's strength was, in reality, his lack of aggression. He was dependable, industrious, and pleasant. He had become Congress's most devoted conservative—not in the sense of right or left, as modern "conservatism" would have it, but in the sense of consistency.

In any disagreement, he would nearly always take the middle position, just in case the winds shifted one way or the other.
It's not that Buchanan wanted to be everyone's buddy; it's just that he frequently made decisions and then rethought them, which irritated even his supposed supporters, particularly Andrew Jackson and James Knox Polk. He frequently resisted running for politics or admitting that he was interested in one or more positions in higher administration.

He was ready to go all-in for the Democratic presidential candidate in 1844, though. His early waffling did him in once more. Buchanan was still unsure whether Pennsylvania's political leaders would consider him ready for the job, so he backed all of the bigwigs without asking for favors.

Meanwhile, Buchanan was dealt another terrible hand by fate. Abel P. Upshur, Secretary of State, was killed by an accidental gun explosion on the USS Princeton on February 28. President Tyler virtually took over the department and, in an attempt to re-elect himself, named expansionist John Calhoun secretary of state and intended to annex Texas. This was tantamount to declaring war on Mexico, but it was welcomed in the South because Texas would almost certainly become a slave state. By mid-April, former President Van Buren had spoken out against the annexation. Henry Clay penned a broadside saying the same thing the same day. It propelled Van Buren back into the contest, because Northern Democrats believed the entire episode and annexation were staged by Southerners to spread slavery.

Van Buren's increasing popularity, combined with the potential of Whigs like Clay supporting him, pushed Buchanan to the rear seat among Northerners. Then, in late May, at the Democratic National Convention, Buchanan and the Pennsylvania delegation fought for, and won, a resolution stating that the presidential candidate needed a two-thirds majority of delegates to be nominated. Because it was a sectional vote, this effectively ended Van Buren's candidacy. Buchanan, who had friends in both the North and the South, appeared to be a good compromise.

The graying mane of Andrew Jackson, the country's most popular politician, then reared its head. He was 77 years old and only a year away from death, but he was still a driving force in the Democratic Party. He had long supported Van Buren, his former vice president, but because Jackson supported annexing Texas, he couldn't allow him to be president. Supporting Buchanan, on the other hand, was never going to happen.

So Jackson chose a neighbor, James Knox Polk, former Speaker of the United States House of Representatives and Governor of Tennessee. It was a calculated operation, with Jackson waiting to see if Van Buren would indeed receive a two-thirds majority at the convention. The conference adjourned for the evening when Van Buren did not win on the first seven ballots. Some Tyler supporters had already abandoned the convention and nominated Tyler to run as a third-party candidate in a rump assembly somewhere in Baltimore.

Polk's name suddenly came up in the conversation the next day, and he gained a few delegates. The New York delegation unexpectedly called for a private conference, and Van Buren withdrew his name before the next ballot, and the convention unanimously voted for Polk, who then nominated vice president Silas Wright, a New Yorker, as a sop to Van Buren. The nomination was then declined by Wright, who was defeated in Pennsylvania by George M. Dallas.

If Jackson had died a year earlier, perhaps 1844 would have been Buchanan's year, but with Polk and Dallas' nominations, Buchanan was trumped twice.

When Polk easily defeated the Whig nominee, Henry Clay, Buchanan wisely wrote to Polk that it was time to reform the Democratic Party. "The old office holders generally have had their day & ought to be content," Buchanan wrote on election day. Polk was still young—he was only forty-nine when elected—so this was definitely intended to flatter the new president, demonstrating that the fifty-three-year-old Buchanan was still thinking young.

Polk had been urged by Jackson to ignore Buchanan's solicitations and perhaps give him something tiny, but Polk eventually succumbed to Buchanan's entreaties and appointed him secretary of state, primarily to open the way for his vice president, Dallas, to take over the Pennsylvania Democrats. Polk, who was finally weaning himself away from Jackson, wanted to make certain that Buchanan—and every other cabinet member—would not be a rival to him.

"Should any member of my Cabinet become a Candidate for the Presidency or Vice Presidency of the United States, it would be expected," Polk wrote to all nominees, "that he will retire from the Cabinet." Polk did not want any patronage that would accumulate into presidential coffers to come from his government. Polk had intimated that he would be a one-term president, but Tyler had also claimed that, and he reneged.

Buchanan, on the other hand, appeared to be content with his high-paying job. "I cheerfully and cordially approve the terms on which this offer has been made," he wrote back to Polk, with one caveat: "I cannot proclaim to the world that in no contingency shall I be a candidate for the Presidency in 1848," but he would certainly resign from the cabinet if that happened.

Buchanan's final address as a senator was a passionate call to annex Texas, which Polk desperately desired. In it, he finally expressed his sentiments regarding slavery, which was the proverbial elephant in the Texas debate. "I am not friendly to slavery in the abstract," he remarked. "I need not say that I have never owned a slave, and I know that I shall never own one... [but] the constitutional rights of the south, under our constitutional compact, are as much entitled to protection as those of any other portion of the Union." He chose slavery and the Union above his personal principles. A few days later, shortly before Polk's inauguration, both houses enacted Texas annexation legislation, and Tyler signed it.

Instead of the purported Great Men of the time, Polk surrounded himself with experts like Buchanan—specialists who could get things done, and done the way Polk wanted them done. Buchanan had overseas diplomatic expertise and, on the side, could handle diplomacy among the Democratic Party's feuding sections in Pennsylvania. For example, financier Robert J. Walker became Secretary of the Treasury, and hawk William L. Marcy of New York was therefore ideal for Polk's expansionist leanings as Secretary of War.

But, before he could do much as secretary of state, Buchanan began making noises about another post. President Tyler had offered Buchanan a seat on the Supreme Court in the spring of 1844, possibly only to get him out of the way of the presidential nomination. Buchanan instantly declined, although it was clear that it had been on his mind for some time. The position, formerly held by Henry Baldwin, who had died, was still open in the fall of 1845, only a few months after Buchanan took over the State Department, and Buchanan went to Polk to express his preference for the Supreme Court post. But he assured Polk that if war broke out with Mexico over Texas, which was a major national and international concern, he would withdraw his proposal.

Polk appeared to be on the verge of agreeing, but Buchanan, as was his custom, changed his mind. He learned that discussions over the Oregon Territory might resume, so he was willing to continue on at the State Department, especially if he could help the Republic gain a few hundred thousand square miles.

Things changed again. There had been no good candidates for the Baldwin Supreme Court seat in the Senate, so Senator Lewis Cass of Michigan, who would later become Buchanan's secretary of state, and Senator Thomas Hart Benton of Missouri informed Polk that Buchanan should have it. Interestingly, Buchanan had only recently been the formal escort at the wedding of Jessie Benton, Thomas' favorite daughter and the bride of John Fremont, who would run against Buchanan as the Republican presidential candidate in 1856. Washington was, and still is, nothing if not incestuous.

So, in order to secure support for his latest seesaw maneuver on the Supreme Court nomination, Buchanan hosted a blowout ball at Carusi's Salon, which was attended by over a thousand of Washington's political and social elite.

Charles Gautier, the most distinguished chef in mid-nineteenth-century America, was hired to cater the event. Gautier was the first of Washington's show-off chefs, comparable to Mario Batali or Anthony Bourdain. Every Christmas, Gautier, who moved from France in 1838 and quickly became the principal distributor of haute cuisine in the United States, would adorn the inside and windows of his Ville de Paris Restaurant at Eleventh Street and Pennsylvania Avenue, a few steps from the White House. Everyone came by, including people who could never afford to eat at the Ville de Paris, to view "a large number of superb Cakes, most tastefully and richly ornamented, ranging in weight from five pounds to nearly twelve hundred pounds!" There were elegantly dressed dolls and various Christmas scenes—one of the capital's major tourist attractions.

The Buchanan celebration on January 23 was extravagant even by Gautier's standards. For the main dishes, there were venison, ham, beef, turkey, pheasant, chicken, oysters, and lobster. Gautier was also a superb confectioner, so he served a dessert buffet that included charlotte russe, fruit and cake pyramids, ice cream, chocolate kisses, and water ice. 300 bottles of wine and 150 bottles of champagne were available.

Though Buchanan was no doubt biting on his fingernails as the tariff discussion raged on, fate intervened. Vice President Dallas, Buchanan's primary opponent in Pennsylvania, would have to break the tie. Dallas was compelled to vote against his state and his strongest supporters in order to fulfill Polk's wishes. Buchanan was never forced to adopt an official stance.

Buchanan's waffling this time put him back on track for the presidency—but not quite yet. The tariff proved to be a passing fad; the North's manufacturing economy did not collapse, and, more importantly, the crisis shifted attention to what was really Polk's New

Democracy goal: to ensure that the United States extended from the Atlantic to the Pacific, and as far north and south as possible.

Buchanan had begun to hate his boss, particularly his edict that no cabinet member should seek the presidency while in office. The only way, Buchanan reasoned, to further his presidential ambitions was to refuse to bow to Polk's requests all the time. Buchanan, for example, changed his opinion three times about what was best in Oregon. When Polk ordered him to advocate for 54/40, Buchanan suggested that he let the British dictate, or at least suggest, the terms. When Polk remarked, "OK, let's go for the 49th parallel," Buchanan responded, "Well, why don't we try for more?" Polk then permitted Buchanan to negotiate for the larger territory without threatening war. Polk let the British dangle for a while before preparing warships to launch hostilities.

At that point, Buchanan had publicly become a strong man to certain Democrats, particularly those who enjoyed significant victories. They were the same people who desired a Mexican war to take over as much territory as possible in that country. Polk was also wary of the war, but he reasoned that it would be difficult to get the land to the Pacific without it. Polk would have been content to split the difference there as well, taking the northern half of California and down to the northern section of New Mexico rather than going all the way south to the Rio Grande River and Baja California. Buchanan, it seemed, would go against Polk under any conditions, and so persuaded him to start a war with Mexico, which he expected to be over in a few months.

What Buchanan did not anticipate, and Polk anticipated, was that initiating the war, with its eventual success, would galvanize the Whigs to put a winning military general at the front of their next presidential ticket. Both Winfield Scott and Zachary Taylor won major wars, resulting in major headlines. Polk had not ruled out running again in 1848, but after the war, despite receiving victory credit, he decided to cut and run. The British had backed down in Oregon, and both parties were satisfied with the forty-ninth parallel as the current border between the United States and Canada. The United States granted the British access to the ports of the Oregon

Territory, allowing cities such as Seattle and Portland on one side and Vancouver and Victoria on the other to grow, particularly with agricultural products from the Northwest available for export.

In the winter, Buchanan began his other strategy, throwing parties every two weeks or so where the booze flowed and presumably the talk flowed in his favor. To be sure, Douglas, to whom he extended invitations each time, did not attend any of them, despite being his presidential rival. The Whigs began to withdraw as well, with Webster willing to back him for the Supreme Court but not for the president. The Pennsylvania delegation was frequently absent as well, as many of them still wanted Vice President Dallas to be promoted.

Cass scored well on the first ballot at the May 1848 convention in Baltimore, prompting Virginia, then a border state leaning away from secession and moving away from slavery itself in many parts, particularly to the west, to leave Buchanan for the Michigander. Taylor, on the other hand, received the Whig candidacy and easily won the election. Buchanan afterwards reflected that he would have been vanquished as well. He believed he would have another chance in 1852. He'd return to Lancaster, make a little money with the law, and wait his turn.

Surprisingly, Buchanan was not sad when he was denied the 1848 nomination.
Buchanan was willing to accept this, but he still believed he was the best civilian politician. He was certainly the most prepared, at least among Democrats, having served in both houses of Congress, in Russia, and as Secretary of State. The Whigs Daniel Webster and Henry Clay could each claim great experience, yet both had previously sought for president and lost. Despite his nomination attempts, Buchanan had no formal loss on his record.

Still, he'd have to figure out a method to pass the time while remaining in the public and political glare. Over the three decades since Buchanan had been there full-time, carriage routes and railroads had made Lancaster considerably more accessible to

Washington, not to mention Baltimore and Philadelphia, so it was hardly going to remain isolated while he devised his idea for 1852.

He purchased the estate in December and moved in after completing his duties as Secretary of State in March 1849. The house and grounds were in fantastic condition, so Buchanan immediately began sending out invitations to politicians to come see the new "Sage of Wheatland," as the journalists had already dubbed him.

Buchanan also looked for methods to maintain himself in the public eye, not necessarily by inflating his resume, but by burnishing it wherever he could. While he did not enjoy his time at Dickinson College, he accepted the challenge of negotiating a peace between students and professors there in 1851. The junior class had rebelled against the rules, and the professors and administration agreed to remove the entire class. Buchanan negotiated a deal in which the students pledged improved behavior in exchange for the faculty letting them back in on the vow to the famous alumnus—a solution not dissimilar to the one his patrons fashioned for him more than thirty years previously.

Marshall College, named for the long-serving Chief Justice of the United States but located in rural Mercersburg, wished to unite with a more centrally placed institution soon after. Buchanan facilitated the union, which took place at Franklin College in Lancaster. He acquired a huge acreage in Wheatland for the new combined institution, made a $1,000 donation to get things going, and was elected chair of the board of trustees. Later, while president, Buchanan rented out Wheatland rooms to Franklin & Marshall students. This was not as mercenary as it seemed on the surface. Buchanan was irritated because Lancaster locals demanded exorbitant rents from Franklin & Marshall young men. He was always an honest trader, undercutting those who were overcharging, but he didn't think it was fair to just give away the rooms. Because he was supporting the institution in the first place, it is likely that he gave whatever he received from his student tenants back to the college, but it would have sounded weird to the public that the sitting president was renting out his property to anyone at all.

Buchanan intended to become a gentleman farmer as well. He had over a thousand strawberry plants and planted trees and ornamental bushes all over the property. During the snowy winter and spring, he enjoyed many sleigh rides and began a new passion of bird-watching in the backwoods. He created a domed wine cellar in the main house's basement and gathered rare vintages. Because the economy was healthy and his investments were doing well, he needed to do little, if any, law work to keep his preferences satisfied.

From his humble origins a few miles to the west, Buchanan had grown into a country squire, with notable visitors, late-night parties, tales exchanged, and cigars smoked. In some ways, this was the pinnacle of his celebrity. There was no pressure to take political positions, even though guests were well aware that he was still interested in the presidency. To be sure, he enjoyed being in the know in Washington, but he was always most at ease in Lancaster, and it didn't take long for him to believe that his acquisition of Wheatland was the best decision he had ever made. He was surrounded by his nieces and nephews, and even if they required his money to survive and thrive, he had no qualms about providing it to them as long as they were thrifty and moving toward good ends.

But there was still one thing missing, and that was undoubtedly the presidency. His recurrent candidacy had become a running gag, particularly among Whigs, of which there were still plenty in central Pennsylvania and adjoining Maryland. Buchanan was not going to let that upset him. He wrote letters late into the night to everyone who might be of service later, so much so that Miss Hetty was afraid his candles would burn him if he fell asleep at his desk.

The country seemed to be in turmoil all the time, and it was nearly always about slavery and where that institution should go. The Missouri Compromise, the Louisiana Purchase, the annexation of Texas, the Mexican War and its peace settlements, the Oregon Territory compromise, the Compromise of 1850, and the Kansas-Nebraska Act were all tangentially related to that fight. Should the slave trade be allowed to continue? Slavery should be allowed in which states? What should be done regarding slaves who have escaped? Could Congress impose restrictions on slavery in the territories? What would it take to keep the Union together if not, as Lincoln lamented, "half slave and half free"?

Buchanan was well aware of every move made in Washington, and what he had done previously was at the heart of everything. If the country had stayed along the Atlantic coast and somewhat inland, as it did when it split from Great Britain, it would have been a minor annoyance. Only when additional states were admitted, changing the composition of Congress, did these concessions become necessary. Even that had been alright for decades following the Missouri Compromise.

The huge acreage gained by the United States as a result of the Mexican War and the Oregon Territory agreement changed everything. The vast majority of the acreage would not be slave land if it were not political. The new territory was unsuitable for crops that required slave labor, and the immensity of the country suited more ambitious and daring men and families.

However, it was political in nature. If the Southern slave states couldn't get enough votes in Congress to keep their slave status, their influence would dwindle dramatically. Modern inhabitants may find it difficult to believe, but slavery was widely accepted throughout the country. Most Southerners wanted it for practical reasons, if not for the racist idea that African Americans were cognitively and morally inferior. Most Northerners ignored the matter. They may have been personally opposed to slavery, but, like a neighbor's tic that they shrugged off, they tolerated slavery in locations where it already existed. There were clearly people who wanted the institution abolished for moral reasons, but they were in the minority.

However, if California joined the Union, there would be one more nonslave state. It seemed obvious that there would be far more free states than slave states in the long term. There had to be a method to appease the slave owners so that slavery was not abolished in a future referendum. The 1850 Compromise was the first attempt.

Although President Taylor was not a supporter of it, he died in office in July 1850, and his successor, Millard Fillmore, a Whig from New

York at the time, pushed it through. The main points of the compromise were as follows: California would be admitted as a free state; Congress would enact a stricter fugitive slave law; the slave trade would be prohibited in the District of Columbia; and Utah and New Mexico would be organized as territories, one on each side of the old Missouri Compromise line of latitude, and they would decide on their slave status when applying for statehood.

It was a massive undertaking, and many believed at the time that it would permanently resolve the nation's main dilemma. Like most such requests, it was clearly a band-aid, and Buchanan was among those who recognized it. But, in order to even consider running for president in 1852, he needed to form a position on the compromise. But, in order to truly distinguish himself from the crowd, he needed to devise a unique reaction.

Buchanan, as he often did, opted to be evasive and convoluted. He mentioned the long-standing Fugitive Slave Law, which dates back to 1793. It was merely that it was only implemented on occasion. Because that was about all the South got out of the bargain, it needed to be better enforced. He was concerned, though, that greater enforcement would excite the individuals he despised the most—rabid anti-slavery abolitionists.

Surprisingly, Buchanan eventually claimed that abolitionists were the ones who instigated the unrest that spilled through Bloody Kansas, secession, and the Civil War. He believed he was the only man who could keep the Union together, and in order to do so, he would have to criticize the abolitionists, whom he believed cared more about destroying slavery than the Union, even if it meant provoking secession.

With that viewpoint, Buchanan attended the 1852 Democratic Convention in Baltimore. Lewis Cass of Michigan and Stephen Douglas of Illinois were his main rivals. The largest delegation, from New York, was led by William Marcy, a fourth favored son contender. The early ballots were dominated by horse trading, with Buchanan leading most of them, but not by nearly enough to secure the nomination. Buchanan made an astute decision. He would have his agents nominate a dark horse who would never really make an impression, and he chose the handsome and young Franklin Pierce of New Hampshire.

Everything backfired. The delegates had it by the forty-ninth ballot. Pierce's freshness invigorated the delegates from New York and Indiana, as well as those from Buchanan's home state of Pennsylvania. The roll call was paused for consultations, and Pierce had received all but 14 of the convention's 296 votes by the end of the ballot.

Buchanan was once again disappointed. He was the finest candidate, and all he received was a consolation prize: the opportunity to nominate his friend, Alabama's William King, as Pierce's running partner. Liberated from the necessity to be "creative" as a candidate, Buchanan became a proponent of the 1850 Compromise as the instrument that could rescue the Union. When Pierce won the election by a landslide, he sought Buchanan's advice, but informed him he wanted new blood, particularly younger men, in the cabinet and higher positions.

Buchanan remained hopeful that he would be able to get something in the cabinet, but it was not to be. He joked with his friends that he had progressed from a middle-aged fogy to an elderly fogy, and that he now had to deal with people no longer calling him "Jimmy" and instead referring to him as "Old Buck." He'd gained weight and his blond hair had become gray. His teeth ached. He was experiencing bilious spasms. His back arched. He was suffering from more hangovers than ever before.

Pierce, on the other hand, was not going to take any chances. He used the Old Hickory playbook and requested that Buchanan be his minister to the United Kingdom. To be sure, Buchanan recognized this was a trick to keep him out of the race for 1856, but he felt honor bound to accept the position after waffling for a long time.

Buchanan's best move while in London was to invite his niece, Harriet, to stay for a while. They charmed the monarchy and higher governmental people together. Although not much came of

Buchanan's visit to Britain, the queen, prime minister, and opposition all had favorable social impressions of the old man with the high collars and his well-educated and well-mannered young ward. As an added advantage, Buchanan was out of the country when every other politician of consequence had to weigh in on the Kansas-Nebraska Act, the pivotal piece of legislation of the day. The fact that he did not state a view on the record kept him out of the conflict, though not entirely above it.

Buchanan was motivated by his time in London. He'd be 65 in 1856, but he wasn't about to give up the twisting route he'd been on for decades. He was going to be Franklin Pierce's successor, by God.

Chapter 3:
The Worst Presidency Commences

Only a few blocks from the magnificent Gateway Arch, St. Louis' most known tourist destination along the Mississippi River, lies a less dramatic and less well-visited companion to that site. The domed edifice, a nineteenth-century architectural masterpiece, is now known as the Historic Old Courthouse.

It was splendid beyond Missouri's influence, signifying "America" in its vast physical stature and the idea that everything in the new country might be as massive as anything before it.

When Roger Brooke Taney took the podium to administer the oath of office to James Buchanan, he was in poor health and elderly age. The new president was only a few weeks away from his sixty-sixth birthday, making him an old man to most of the country, but the long-faced, long-haired, dour-looking Taney was days away from his eightieth birthday.

He, too, was a Dickinson College graduate, having arrived at the age of fifteen. He was the second son of tobacco farmers in Calvert County, Maryland, just across the Mason-Dixon Line in Maryland, a slave state where Pennsylvania was not, and his family had a huge crew of slaves because tobacco was a big slave-oriented crop.

As the sky darkened during the Buchanan inauguration—the weather began springlike but would change to snow by evening—Taney met briefly with Buchanan before the ceremony began. Buchanan had opted to have his inauguration speech printed, at least in part, so that everyone in the audience would have something to remember him by. Some retailers even had it printed on silk.

However, two elements of the speech that Buchanan really delivered were not included in the printed mementos. One example was Buchanan's promise to serve only one term. The other was a few cryptic phrases stating that the Supreme Court will issue a ruling shortly determining how slavery would be adjudicated in the territories, and that Buchanan was convinced it would save the Union.

Taney undoubtedly informed Buchanan that the verdict will be made public soon. Some believe it happened during his brief conversation with a fellow Dickinson alum on the podium, as evidenced by the additional words in his speech.

Even if Taney had informed Buchanan about the decision's scheduling earlier, Buchanan already knew what the outcome of the justices' decision—the one involving the country's most famous slave, Dred Scott—would be.

James Buchanan had not waited to take office before starting the carousel of the worst administration in American history.
The Dred Scott case had been circling the courts for more than a decade when it was eventually heard and decided by the Supreme Court. Because so many facts in the case had changed dramatically in the interim—Scott's owner dying, his former master's family funding his appeal, Scott alternating between being free and slave— the court may hear it narrowly or widely. If it had decided narrowly, for example, it might have found a technicality to hang Scott's freedom or captivity on without impacting most others.

Buchanan, like Taney, believed the case should end with a sweeping decision that would put an end to the debate over slavery for good. If the Supreme Court ordered it, it would take precedence above party politics. People and politicians might moan or object, but, according to the two Dickinson graduates, it would be done and the country could move on.

Except Buchanan wanted to ensure that the nation saw it as a Washington consensus. If the vote was five to four, it would look to be simply another Southern partisan bargain, no more sustaining than any of the previous compromises, provisos, or acts.

When it came to the Constitution, Buchanan had always asserted that whatever else the United States was, it was first and foremost a union founded on the ideas established by the Founding Fathers three quarters of a century before his presidency. Nonetheless, in January 1857, two months before taking office, Buchanan wrote a note to his friend Associate Justice John Catron, who had come from Tennessee, wondering how the Dred Scott debates were progressing.

Knowing that the decision was imminent, Buchanan apparently added a section to his inaugural address stating that the question of whether those voting in the territories could reject or assent to slavery truly belonged "to the Supreme Court of the United States, before whom it is now pending, and will, it is understood, be swiftly and finally settled." I will cheerfully submit to their decision, as will all good citizens, whatever it may be, though it has always been my personal opinion that, under the Nebraska-Kansas Act, the appropriate period will be when the number of actual residents in the Territory shall justify the formation of a constitution with a view to its admission as a State into the Union."

As tolerant as most Americans were of slavery, at least in the South, the legalization of it in Dred Scott infuriated Northerners and even perplexed Southern Unionists. Taney's phrasing was harsh. Black people, not only slaves, were "unfit to associate with the White race," he said in the ruling, "and so far inferior that they had no rights which the white man was bound to respect."

Almost soon, the country descended into a greater schism than had ever been witnessed. Southerners were relieved. They believed that Buchanan, their Doughface lackey in the White House, had preserved the Union. Not only was their territory safe for slavery, but they no longer risked losing their slaves through escape because they would always be slaves regardless of where they ended up. Northerners, both Democrat and Republican, were furious because their states were now practically slave states. They didn't want anything to do with it, especially working men whose pay depended on not having slave labor competition. There was also the added complication that Northerners, rather than just ignoring the Fugitive Slave Law, would now face prosecution if they did not. It also looked to leave open the possibility of Kansas becoming a slave state, because the Missouri Compromise line was no longer legitimate, and with Buchanan essentially identifying himself with the South, slaveholders would grow more daring and figure out a method to force slavery to happen in Kansas.

The Dred Scott ruling also galvanized a hitherto marginalized group: abolitionists. They believed that the only way to stop the expansion of slavery was to abolish it entirely, and they now had a flag to rally behind. More traditional Democrats felt misled. Stephen Douglas's key issue of "popular sovereignty," in which settlers would decide whether or not to have slavery once their region became a state, had died. With the deaths of Henry Clay and Daniel Webster several years before, Thomas Hart Benton, possibly the most respected man in Congress, produced a book criticizing the judgment, with all sorts of precedents and other arguments against it, which became a smash seller. Almost every Northern newspaper, whether Democrat, Republican, or Know-Nothing, opined against Dred Scott.

The reaction perplexed Buchanan. He imagined it was the "new" compromise, replacing Missouri, which he considered out of date because so much area had been added to the country since then. This would give the country time to let slavery die naturally, rather than in a cataclysm.

It had only taken two days for Buchanan to commit a major error. Nonetheless, in the period before taking office, he had already laid the groundwork for many more.

For decades in Pennsylvania, Buchanan did one thing well: he served as the point man for conciliation. He was not adored in Pennsylvania, but he was respected, especially when he demonstrated to old and new adversaries that the Democratic Party could only survive in a swing state at the time if it was more or less united. He acknowledged that diverse points of view will always exist on some subjects, but he believed that dissent would strengthen the party even more.

But when it came to choosing a cabinet, Buchanan concluded that this was not the way to go. As Secretary of State under President James Knox Polk, Buchanan had been a dissenting cabinet member. He knew Polk did not consider him one of his favorites, and they frequently disagreed, but he felt he provided Polk something by expressing his opposing viewpoints.

Whether by intent or by chance, Buchanan chose a cabinet that would not disagree with him significantly. Franklin Pierce would be the only president to have the same cabinet for all four years of his presidency. Buchanan may have considered that having a cabinet with a single voice was a good thing.

Buchanan's cabinet was mostly made up of Southerners or other Doughfaces like him. Nobody should have been surprised, given that Buchanan had spent almost all of his time in Washington working and partying with Southerners, and given how long he had been there, it would have been a huge shock to assume he would not sympathize with them. There was no opponent or great thinker among his selections, and even the cabinet's seeming regional diversity was a ruse.

Howell Cobb was always a favorite of Buchanan's. He had a thousand slaves on his Georgia farm, despite his long hair and chubbiness. He was a political dynamo, becoming Speaker of the House at the age of thirty-four, then governor of Georgia before returning to Congress. He was reportedly Buchanan's key advisor in selecting his cabinet, of which he became Secretary of the Treasury. Cobb was lauded as a Unionist, yet being a Unionist and a slaveholder meant wanting slavery to spread across the territories and Northerners to accept it. As a result, he was a strong backer of the 1850 Compromise and, later, the Dred Scott judgment.

Simply put, Buchanan despised Douglas. Douglas nearly ruined Buchanan's last chance to run for president by staying in the campaign until the last minute at the 1856 convention. However, Buchanan did not learn from his previous political idol, Andrew Jackson. Jackson discovered something for everyone he needed to control. Jackson sent Buchanan to Russia to keep him out of the presidential race, but he did allow Buchanan to achieve his goal of negotiating the first trade deal with Czar Nicholas.

Douglas received nothing from Buchanan. Douglas did not admire Buchanan as much as the president did, but he was pragmatic and actively supported Buchanan's campaign. When Buchanan declared that he would be a one-term president, Douglas became the clear front-runner for 1860, and he was free to court or defy Buchanan as he saw fit for his possible campaign. He was the most popular senator in the North, or at least the Northwest, and the Democrats needed him to win in 1860.

Buchanan was especially enraged that Douglas, a widower, had married Adele Cutts, a young Washington beauty. After Mrs. Douglas's father applied for a job in the administration, Buchanan wrote to a friend that if he approved the appointment, "it will be my own regard for Mr. Cutts and his family, and not because Senator Douglas has had the good fortune to become his son-in-law." Even Buchanan's one move to thank Douglas for his support during the 1856 election was snide—the letter he wrote in thanks was addressed to "The Hon. Samuel A. Douglas," the first-name mix-up most likely not an error.

Essentially, this friendly cabinet would be bad as well. Buchanan had always valued consensus and would seek it even beyond hours. These were also social acquaintances of the president. The cabinet would convene almost every day for several hours. Then Buchanan, a lonely guy without a family, would invite some or all of them over for supper at night, frequently with wives and family members present if they were available. It was both an honor and an annoyance—no one would ever leave the office.

That resulted in a fairly congealed and close group, but it also meant that no one could tell Buchanan when he went off the rails, as he was prone to do. He would frequently hesitate on significant subjects, and might easily end up on the most rash side of them.

I idled over some of the displays in the cases when I arrived at the neighborhood coin shop, which was crowded. I was drawn to a series of coins from the mid-nineteenth century. There were huge coins throughout the 1840s and 1850s, up until the coins of 1857, which were just half the size of the others.

"Oh, the Panic of 1857," the owner remarked when I inquired about the size shift. "It was terrible. The president does not appear to have a remedy other than using less gold or silver in the coins."

That president, of course, was James Buchanan, and his minimalist answer to one of America's major economic downturns was about as anemic as it could be.

In truth, the country had been doing well for a long time before Buchanan effectively caused the 1857 Panic.

There had been a catastrophic slump twenty years before, with numerous causes such as war in Europe, the breakup of the Federal Reserve Bank of the United States, and overspeculation in, strangely, slaves, corn, and Western land. Polk's massive property acquisitions from Oregon to California to Texas re-energized the economy, and the boom lasted at least a decade. Because so many people desired to go west into new territories and states, railroads were the primary mode of transportation. Manufacturing expanded both locally and internationally, as Europe had ended many of its hostilities and American goods were cheaper than those on the Continent.

The Tariff Bill of 1857, passed the day before Buchanan assumed office, cut duties on a wide range of imported commodities (Buchanan intended to boost foreign trade), but rendered American manufactured goods less competitive.

By July, no one could ride the Reading, as Uncle Pennybags does in the Monopoly game, because it had closed down, as had other historic lines like the Illinois Central. Several railroads declared bankruptcy, including the Delaware, Lackawanna, and Western and the Fond du Lac Railroad in Wisconsin.

Thousands of people were laid off, and banks began foreclosing on loans and property. Senator William Seward, the new Republican Party's leader, returned from vacation to discover that he had lost almost everything he possessed; his stock in the Illinois Central, recommended to him by his Democratic opponent Stephen Douglas, was virtually worthless. Every bank in New York City virtually shut down—no one would exchange coins or gold for banknotes. The oldest grain company in New York, N. H. Wolfe and Company went bankrupt in August, as did the country's most important insurance company, the Ohio Life Insurance and Trust Company.

The sinking of the SS Central America in a hurricane in September 1857 was uncontrollable, but it did not improve matters. The ship was carrying 30,000 pounds of gold from the California gold rush and was on its way up to New York when it encountered what is now known as a Category 2 hurricane, with gusts of up to 105 miles per hour, off the coast of North Carolina. More than 400 people died on board, and the entire cargo of gold plummeted to the bottom of the sea.

While the loss of the gold, which was worth around $2 million at the time, would not have been disastrous to the economy if Buchanan and the government had done nothing to calm the public outrage provoked by the sinking. Calm words may have calmed it down, but it just led to further bank runs and, as a result, more market instability.

The most important remnant, however, was the reaction generated by Dred Scott. Instead of strengthening unity and opening up the West to additional settlement, as Buchanan had hoped, Dred Scott stymied it, thereby ending years of Northern prosperity.

However, the South did not fare as severely. Its agrarian culture was self-sufficient, and its cotton was still sold in Europe. Northerners accused Buchanan of being a Southern lackey as a result.

His reaction was disappointing, almost dismissive. He said that the federal government was powerless to intervene. Even his supporter, writer Philip Klein, acknowledged Buchanan's heartlessness.

Buchanan outlined his policy in his December 1857 Annual Message: reform, not relief. The government sympathized but could do nothing to ameliorate people's misery. It would continue to fulfill its commitments in gold and silver; it would not cut back on public works but would not start any new ones... Buchanan's personal view was that men who respected property would not put it to work unless it was backed up by solid collateral; those who took the speculative risk deserved the destiny of a gambler. In the case of the innocent victims, tenacity would triumph over adversity, and the buoyancy of youth and the energy of the people would allow them to recover. The forecast came true, but not before uncountable thousands of people faced the agony of broken lives, impending famine, and despair.

The economy would not fully recover until, sadly, a few years later, it had to supply a national war.

However, Buchanan's year of infamy did not conclude with "broken lives, imminent starvation, and despair" caused by a failing economy. He had at least one more crisis to start. The Mormons were not a popular group, but the federal government, under Millard Fillmore and Franklin Pierce, tried to ignore them and let them build their Zion in the wastelands of Utah Territory. Brigham Young, the Mormon leader, was the governor, and he seemed to merely want to be left alone, which was acceptable with most Americans considering what was going on with slavery and the like.

However, in 1857, Mormon settlers wanted to begin the process of creating a state while also protesting that federal judges in the territory were dishonest and attempting to swindle people off their land. In the other direction, the judges said that Mormons were seizing and destroying federal documents, rendering the judges unable to do their duties.

Without investigating any of this, Buchanan named a new governor, Alfred Cumming, and ordered 2,500 men, a large number for the period, led by Colonel Albert Sidney Johnson, later a notable Confederate general, to go defend American law in this wastrel state.

Needless to say, the maneuvers infuriated Young and his constituents, as well as Kansas Governor Walker, who would be losing the Johnson troops to what appeared to him to be a futile mission. He persuaded Buchanan to relent and leave some of the cavalry in Kansas, but Johnson and the rest of the army fled.

Meanwhile, Young had never received the letter informing him that he had been succeeded as governor. It was a Pierce blunder this time, with Buchanan's predecessor canceling the Utah mail contract. To be sure, Buchanan had no intention of resurrecting it.

Young, hearing only that a massive federal force was on its way to shut him down, organized his own army and ordered them to burn everything—every building, every tree, every hay bale—that the federal force may take on its way to the anticipated invasion.

Mormons allegedly massacred innocent wagon trains of people and animals traveling west, and the federal brigade was assaulted multiple times in the final miles, losing cattle and troops.

Thomas L. Kane of Philadelphia, one of Buchanan's old acquaintances, learned about this horrific blunder and volunteered himself as a freelance diplomat because he had previously associated with several Mormons. Buchanan agreed but did not pay Kane's wages or cover his costs. By the time Kane arrived and calmed things down, thousands of Mormons had lost their homes and livelihoods, flaming everything as Young had instructed and fleeing the army.

Buchanan provided his standard solution—not much. He granted the Mormons amnesty in exchange for submission to federal law, but there was little hope of continuing the process toward statehood (Utah did not become a state until 1896). For their own safety, the troops stayed, albeit forty miles distant. It took another year for the Mormons to return to their charred lands and begin rebuilding their lives after losing everything due to Buchanan's overreaction to what would have been a minor administrative matter.

The first year of America's worst administration had come to an end.

Chapter 4:
The Middle Buchanan Presidency

When he entered the Senate floor on May 19, 1856, Massachusetts senator Charles Sumner was hardly a dove on the question of slavery. He was to make an oration on the looming problem in Kansas, a sparsely inhabited territory west of Missouri and primarily beyond the Missouri Compromise's barrier separating slave states from those intended to be free.

It wasn't his first address on the subject in his five years in the Senate, but it was his most memorable. He decided to utilize sexual comparisons to rail against Slave Power, the slave-owning group in the South most prominent in attempting to inflict slavery on Kansas: "This uncommon tragedy did not have its origin in any common lust for power." It is the rape of a virgin Territory, subjecting it to the heinous embrace of slavery; and it can be plainly linked back to a perverted yearning for a new Slave State, the monstrous child of such a crime, in the aim of increasing the influence of slavery in the National Government."

Kansas had become a mini-California by the mid-1850s. Although there was no gold or an ocean, as in California, Kansas possessed millions of acres of land, the majority of which was arable and ready for business.

Stephen Douglas was the chair of the Senate Committee on Territories, and as such, he was the creative genius in figuring out how to include them into the American dream. In theory, his Kansas-Nebraska Act could have been a stroke of genius. It offered two potential states, Kansas and Nebraska, and stated that they would be able to choose whether to be slave or free upon admission to the Union.

Douglas was well aware that Kansas was unsuitable for slavery, that its land was unsuitable for cotton, tobacco, or any other crop typically slave-honed in the South. Thus, he reasoned, a choose-your-own-status plan could appease the South without endangering the North, that the two states would eventually become free, but that Southerners, too, may begin settling there—and possibly giving up their slaves in the process.

In theory, and with bipartisan support, Douglas' act was a nonstarter in actuality. As settlers arrived, many of whom came from slave-holding Missouri across the border, two governmental centers were founded. The one in Lecompton, which formed first, defended slavery, and the one in Topeka, which formed soon after, advocated for Kansas to be a free state.

In Kansas, there were battles between different types of settlers, individuals died at random, and a lot of others were scared off. The most notable event was the Pottawatomie Creek massacre, which occurred two days after Brooks' beating of Sumner. John Brown, a man regarded as half-crazed even by some of his friends, and a gang of seven others, including his three sons, allegedly murdered five supposed slave sympathizers and cut their bodies into at least some sections afterwards.

With the territory in turmoil, Buchanan was forced to devise a novel solution. One of the better ideas could have been to appoint Stephen Douglas as governor of Kansas, a position he would have gladly accepted. Douglas created the situation, and perhaps he would have worked hard to resolve it.

Buchanan, on the other hand, would not have been happy if Douglas had actually proposed a remedy. He despised the senator from Illinois so much. If Douglas could have solved Kansas, or even stopped the strife there, he would have presumably returned to the Senate if Kansas became a state. He'd be a foregone conclusion as the Democratic presidential candidate in 1860, with a good possibility of being the hero who held the country together, something Buchanan could not contemplate.

Buchanan did appoint a capable individual. Robert Walker, a native Pennsylvanian, was valedictorian of his class at the University of Pennsylvania before becoming a lawyer and moving to Mississippi to join his brother. He became a wealthy planter and slaveholder, then a senator from his adopted state, before becoming Secretary of the Treasury under President James Knox Polk, when he became friendly with Buchanan. After the Polk administration, he retired to practice law and appeared to be the right kind of nonpartisan man to lead things in Kansas after a string of ineffective governors.

That might have been the case if Buchanan had opted to listen to Walker. Buchanan appeared to believe that the Lecompton group was the real territorial administration, on the basis of first come, first served.

Walker saw through the ploy and sought to persuade Buchanan that it was a better idea to make Kansas a free state, given that there were only a dozen or so slaves in Lecompton. Buchanan did not believe Walker's advice. Both the Topeka and Lecompton governments claimed validity, and the only way to resolve the issue, according to Buchanan, was for voters to vote on the Lecompton constitution, the first of the two designs. "On the question of submitting the Constitution to bona fide residents of Kansas, I am willing to stand or fall," Buchanan wrote to Walker.

Incongruously, Lecompton proudly promotes itself as the "Civil War Birthplace" and hosts annual events commemorating "Bleeding Kansas." It celebrates, fairly or unfairly, the voting on the Lecompton constitution, which not only permitted slavery in Kansas, but made it an inalienable right until at least 1864, when, presumably, Kansas would have long been a state and its legacy would have been too entrenched to remove.

The majority of anti-slavery citizens stayed at home for the Lecompton election, which was primarily about whether slavery would be permitted in a possible state of Kansas. Northerners from both parties were angry that Buchanan was pushing for such an election. To them, any election had to be about the entire constitution, which they believed was utterly illegal because it was promulgated by a slave-supporting administration that excluded the majority of the rest of the population. The fact that a referendum later revealed that 10,226 Kansans were against the entire Lecompton constitution, with less than 200 in favor—implying a desire on the part of most Kansans to just start over—did not appear to sway Buchanan.

With the Lecompton constitution, Buchanan placed his reputation as a negotiator on the line, submitting it to Congress entirely, with the slavery cause and the manifestly invalid local vote intact. The Senate, which is predominantly Democratic and Southern, would pass the bill, but the House was deadlocked. Buchanan put his cabinet and other advisors to work, offering land grants and other perks to the on-the-fence representatives—despite charges that some of those proposals were bribes and even secret sexual favors from prostitutes.

In the end, the bill was defeated in the House, and a new, properly constructed constitution was established in Kansas, which became a state just as the Civil War began in 1861—a free state, but with as much animosity as any other before or after.

Buchanan's failed bid was widely interpreted as evidence of his Southern sympathies. The 1858 fall congressional elections were a colossal failure. Democrats were defeated by Republicans in New York, New Jersey, Ohio, Indiana, New England, and even Pennsylvania, with the most severe defeat coming from Pennsylvanian J. Glancy Jones, Buchanan's most devoted workhorse in the House.

At the very least, Buchanan accepted responsibility, writing to his niece Harriet, "Well! "We've met the enemy," he added, "and we're theirs." This is something I've been looking forward to for three months." Even though the Democrats had a nominal majority, there would be little from the Buchanan White House that would be readily passed once the new Congress convened in 1859.

As Kansas and the Panic sucked the life out of any glimmer of hope for the still-young government, Buchanan tried to press on with what he saw as his specialty: expanding the United States as far as possible.

While serving as the envoy to England during the Pierce administration, he and the ministers to France and Spain met in secret to devise a plan to include Cuba into the American republic.

The document they handed to President Franklin Pierce was named the Ostend Manifesto, after the location in Belgium where they convened, and was most likely composed entirely by Buchanan based on its phraseology.

Slavery was the overarching motive for Doughfaces like Buchanan and Pierce to add Cuba to the list of states. Slaves already predominated in Cuba, accounting for roughly one-third of the million persons counted in the 1850 census. If admitted to the Union at that point, Cuba would have not only the two senators required by the Constitution, but also nine members of the House of Representatives, which would be a lot of voting power.

By the end of the Pierce administration, the Ostend Manifesto had become one of the most powerful rallying cries for the abolitionist movement. It was openly aimed at bolstering Southern slavocracy, and when Slave Power organizations began to advocate for it with force, it merely invigorated the exact people Buchanan feared, the radical anti-slavery groups.

Despite this, Buchanan was continuously looking for ways to annex or conquer Cuba during his presidency, especially in its early years, when he still had some support among Northern Democrats. He'd try to persuade them that appeasing the South wasn't such a horrible idea, especially if it meant saving the Union, and Cuba was an easy target. He offered that one of his bargaining chips with Spain be cash, which the US almost certainly possessed, and that the slave trade itself be abolished.

Buchanan also envisioned the Great Republic expanding into Mexico and Central America—Manifest Destiny 2.0. William Walker, the most renowned of the potential conquerors known as "filibusters," rolled over Nicaragua twice, seeking to either become its ruler or deliver it to Buchanan as a slave state.

Buchanan sent troops down to capture Walker and his mercenaries only for show. When Commodore Hiram Paulding took Walker back to New Orleans to face charges, Buchanan denied Walker's detention, claiming it had occurred unlawfully on foreign soil, and censured Paulding. Walker, on the other hand, got his comeuppance. He returned to Nicaragua, expecting to seem as a rescuer, but was slain by villagers who were clearly tired of him and the Buchanan administration in general.

Buchanan also advocated for petty—perhaps even ridiculous—wars in the hopes of gaining favor with expansionists, a group that had dwindled by the time Kansas had exhausted everyone. He fought in the now-forgotten Pig War in the Strait of Juan de Fuca, off the Olympic Peninsula.

In what was plainly a minor incident, Buchanan despatched General Winfield Scott with troops and warships on a six-week voyage from New York to the strait through Panama. By the time Scott arrived, men and ships were ready to fire at each other over, well, a pig. Scott, a former Whig who was never a fan of Buchanan in the first place, recommended a non-hostile occupation of the strait, which lasted another decade. Scott couldn't figure out what Buchanan expected to happen—perhaps additional territory and a stronger harbor in the Northwest—but he wasn't about to risk it with his fatigued troops over some swine-shooting settlers.

Buchanan's invasion of Paraguay in 1859 was at least as humiliating and wasteful. Paraguay, yes. The fledgling former Spanish colony claimed territory that it claimed was seized by American Americans living there. And, to be honest, it did conduct one heinous crime: it opened fire on an American ship inspecting the rivers of the landlocked country, killing an officer.

Buchanan despatched 2,500 marines and nineteen warships to South America, where they traveled up the Parana River to the Paraguayan capital of Asuncion. By the time they arrived, even the most fervent expansionists and slaveholding firebrands who might have thought Paraguay was ripe for a slave state were not on board with

Buchanan's invasion. As a result, the expedition turned around nearly immediately, taking several months to return intact.

"In the meantime, these men and ships could have been employed in reinforcing American coastal forts, where they were needed to prevent attacks by seceding southern states, rather than fending off distant insults to the flag," Jean Baker noted in her not always favorable biography of Buchanan. Instead, the government's inadequate response merely encouraged secession."

The latter years of Buchanan's presidency were not much better, if at all, than his first. He did have some work to do in his final months in office, though, to cement his legacy as the Worst. President. Ever.

Chapter 5:
Mr. Buchanan's War

When the Civil fight's anniversary — and possibly tercentennial — arrives years from now, there will still be people who argue that the fight was all about "states' rights" and little about slavery. They would argue that the Confederate flag is merely a banner for individuals who identify with Southern culture, no more dangerous than a high school mascot, and far from a sign of a society that believed people of one skin color were so far inferior to those of another that they should have been treated as chattel.

If they could transport themselves back to the early 1860s, they would discover that the only state right mentioned in any Southern secession document was related to the institution of slavery, and that the only thing that separated the majority of the people in each section of the country was their laws concerning slavery.

True, most white people, North and South, including the man in the White House in 1860, James Buchanan, were convinced that black people were not as competent in most ways as whites, but in the Northern part of the country—and in the lands of the West moving toward statehood—they believed that a free market system, with all laborers earning some sort of income, was far superior to slavery.

At the time of the Buchanan presidency, the average Southerner's economic and social standing lagged well behind that of his northern counterparts. According to the 1850 United States census, there were 2,399,651 native-born whites in New England, with just 6,209 of those over the age of twenty unable to read or write. In Virginia, however, there were around one-third the number of native-born whites—871,847—and twelve times the number of illiterates aged twenty and up, or 75,863 people. In comparison to the states to its south, Virginia was an intellectual haven. Ten percent of white adults in Arkansas were illiterate, as did 15% in North Carolina. In his fundamental account of the pre-Civil War era, Ordeal of the Union, historian Allan Nevins writes, "School appropriations were wretched, and it was said that even penal laws would hardly compel many rural parents to put their children into classes."

The South's financial triumph may have been false, but its pride was real. Southern slaveholders' pride became somewhat protective as their influence waned. The slave owners could add Texas to their list, but with the failure of Kansas and the failure of any of Buchanan's efforts into Cuba and Central America, they would have to stay where they were.

If Buchanan didn't see it right away, he certainly did after Kansas. Nonetheless, he would go to any extent to appease his southern buddies. At every point, he blamed the increasing abolitionist movement in the North for worsening the sectional conflict. The assumption was that if slaveholders were left alone, the institution could fade down, but it would be confined, as the past big concessions had provided. Once anti-slavery activists got going, they only enraged the South. It was a point of view he never changed, and his final memoirs, released after the Civil War, emphasized it.

After the 1858 midterm elections, Buchanan had nothing left to recover. Stephen Douglas, his fiercest political foe, was the only significant Northern victory in his party. Despite helping to create a new national political celebrity, Republican Abraham Lincoln, by holding debates with him during the Illinois Senate election, Douglas still won. Though William Seward remained the overwhelming favorite to win the Republican candidate in 1860, Lincoln's loss by Douglas undoubtedly improved his prospects.

For the remainder of Buchanan's presidency, he would have a difficult time getting anything major passed via a Congress that was mostly made up of Republicans or Southern Democrats who were growing increasingly impatient to either separate or receive concessions that were probably no longer achievable. Buchanan proposed little but continued to hold endless cabinet meetings virtually daily, with little give-and-take. One cabinet debate so irritated his friend, Treasury Secretary Howell Cobb, that Cobb quipped that Buchanan's waffling drove him to "oppose the administration."

If Buchanan wanted to leave a most somber legacy—saving the Union—he needed to make peace with Douglas. If he could achieve that and get the Democratic Party a strong and unifying candidate in 1860, he'd be able to return to Wheatland relatively unscathed. Buchanan may not have wanted to do it on his own, but he had long kept the Pennsylvania Democrats at least relatively cordial, so it was possible.

The issue became that the individuals Buchanan listened to the most feared Douglas would seek vengeance on them if he was elected. Cobb and the other Southerners in his cabinet, as well as lawmakers such as Mississippi's Jefferson Davis and Georgia's Alexander Stephens, had Buchanan's ear. Buchanan plainly perceived the 1858 elections and the North's unification around the Republican movement as a rejection of him by the entire country. He disliked New Englanders, for example, and although having visited Scotland, Paris, and St. Petersburg, he had never visited Hartford or the Green Mountains, despite spending a little time there as secretary of state with Polk.

He used to be a Doughface, but after living in the Southern-leaning metropolis of Washington for so long, he was practically a Southerner. Whatever they thought of him personally, Southerners backed him politically. He realized he would have to stand by them as well.

Whatever Buchanan did, however, always appeared to backfire, even though it should not have touched him in the first place. Daniel Sickles, who had held numerous political positions in New York, was Buchanan's secretary (basically his chief of staff) while he was minister to Great Britain. Sickles, then thirty-three, married fifteen-year-old Teresa Bagioli and got her pregnant a few months before leaving for London; he subsequently abandoned her. Fanny White, a notorious prostitute he "studied with" in New York, accompanied him to Great Britain, and he even introduced her to Queen Victoria in court.

Buchanan was chastised for visiting Sickles, who was definitely a buddy from their time serving together in London. It is unknown whether any other sitting president visited a friend in jail, but journalists, particularly those critical of him, questioned why he had not, for example, visited imprisoned slaves or employees in debtors' prisons.

Few, however, ever argued that Buchanan received bribes or was otherwise politically corrupt. Others in his administration could not be considered to be the same. When the Republicans took control of Congress in the middle of Buchanan's term, they appointed a fellow Pennsylvanian, John Covode, known as "Honest John," to form a committee to investigate any bribes Buchanan may have used to get Kansas's Lecompton constitution passed.

Without a doubt, there is proof that Buchanan's cabinet was corrupt long before the Kansas affair. Secretary of War John Floyd was involved in a number of dubious transactions. The government frequently overpaid for real estate for its forts and armories, particularly from Democratic contributors, and then awarded sweetheart contracts for construction. It paid a low price for Fort Snelling, a large piece of land near the Mississippi River in Minnesota, to a partnership of Virginia Democrats, and frequently purchased armaments, some of which were antiquated, from fraudulent companies. Montgomery Miegs, a Washington-based army officer who protested about all this fraud, was sent to the Dry Tortugas off the coast of Florida—not a vacation destination at the time, as it may be later—to keep his voice away from prosecutors ears. The enormous rosters of port agents and postmasters were also ripe for graft. While some of the patronage employees in such positions did their tasks, there was too little work for the amount of appointees, thus the administration had hundreds of no-work, full-pay jobs available.

The committee refused to let Buchanan defend himself or even testify, and Buchanan urged the committee to impeach him if they truly believed he had committed an illegal act. When the investigation was completed, Buchanan declared that he had "passed triumphantly through this ordeal," but he was plainly embarrassed, his entire government seeming weak and, at best, complicit, if not dishonest.

Buchanan had long promised a scandal-free administration, pledging that if anything smelt even slightly crooked, he would deal with it right away. Politics, however, took care of that in the end. By the halfway of his presidency, he concluded that the best legacy he could leave was to leave the Union whole. The only way for it to happen today was for him to appease the Southerners in his cabinet and party. If he went after those like Floyd or Secretary of the Interior Jacob Thompson, who allegedly benefitted from the numerous Kansas vote bribes, he would be "insulting" Southerners, giving them even more incentive to leave not just the party, but the Union.
So the stage was set for the last act. The Fat Lady's quavering warble had almost arrived.

It was obvious that Brown was planning an attack someplace. He had met the most prominent figures in the abolitionist movement, from Harriet Tubman to William Lloyd Garrison to Frederick Douglass, in public, not behind closed doors, and Tubman, at the very least, assisted him in his search for slaves who would want to join his insurrection. Brown had received donations of munitions and money from all over the North, and had he not been pursued by the pro-slavery folks he met in Kansas, he would have been easy to trace.

Nonetheless, Buchanan let him ride. The president primarily regarded the American army as responsible for safeguarding settlers in the West, rather than other domestic problems. According to historical estimates, the army in the decade preceding the Civil War had around sixteen thousand troops, therefore Buchanan may not have had much choice but to play it safe. It may have been too much to expect Buchanan to have extra troops at Harper's Ferry, but neglecting such a well-known figure as Brown was a mistake.

Even after Brown struck Harper's Ferry, it took Buchanan two days to bring a company of marines to Brown's makeshift "fort," which was essentially an armory building in which he was confined and surrounded by local farmers and workers. Even so, Buchanan was fortunate that then-Colonel Robert E. Lee was in Washington on leave from his regular duties in Texas.

Buchanan then stepped back and allowed Virginia politicians to take charge. If he had ordered Brown's relocation to Washington or another more neutral prison and presided over an orderly trial, the incident could have been avoided. The president, on the other hand, delegated oversight to pro-slavery men who, although following the general rules of free trials, permitted Brown's case to become a controversial event. Brown was convicted quickly, despite the fact that it was conceded that he never killed anyone or freed any slaves, the offenses for which he was charged. He was not allowed to use the insanity argument that Buchanan's pal Sickles used in his blatant murder of Philip Key.

By the time Brown was hanged in nearby Charles Town on December 2, 1859, he had become a cause célèbre unlike any other in American history. The literary sages of the time, Ralph Waldo Emerson, Victor Hugo, Henry David Thoreau, and Walt Whitman, all wrote about Brown, if not in glowing terms, then in sympathy, and anticipated war as a result of his raid and its consequences. During the execution, about 2,000 soldiers arrived to safeguard the town from a riot.

Buchanan's nightmare was looming. The slave debate, which he had believed would die, became ferocious. Many Northerners who had previously supported slavery now saw it as a moral blight on America, the country they believed would show the rest of the world how to live.

Yet, as the song goes, Buchanan carried on as if John Brown's body were not "a-mouldering in the grave." Saving the Union seemed to rate lower than settling old scores.

Buchanan was still the Democratic Party's nominal leader, and as such had the final say on where the 1860 nominating convention would be held. Elbert B. Smith, a historian at the University of

Maryland, stated in his 1975 book The Presidency of James Buchanan:

In Washington, Buchanan sat motionless while the convention committed party suicide. Instead of trying to acquire its nominee first and then develop a platform for him to run on, it came up with a Buchanan-advised platform that could not possibly be friendly to his opponent and projected candidacy, Stephen Douglas. There were a few minor items on the program, but generally, the party would be dedicated to allowing slavery in the territories and to backing the country's expansion to Cuba and Central America, both of which were presumably slave areas.

Buchanan would not bend in his efforts to persuade his Southern allies otherwise. One argument was that they made the platform so onerous for Northern Democrats that they would either seek a Southern replacement for Douglas or accept the Southerners defecting and supporting a rival candidate. Unionists in the South assumed the election would be thrown to the House, which would not find a majority candidate. The Senate would then choose a Southern vice president to succeed him as president.

For those of practical mind who longed for the country's unity, the few months of the 1860 campaign were a blur of impassioned rhetoric and pain. With the Democrats so deeply divided, no amount of mocking and vilifying the new Republican hero, Abraham Lincoln, would influence the outcome of the electoral college. Lincoln was never the favorite, but his handlers outmaneuvered every other candidate at the party's raucous Chicago convention, including the primary candidate, William Seward, who had patiently waited his turn in the first Republican election in 1856. Seward, ever practical, instantly endorsed Lincoln, for which Lincoln would repay the favor by not only appointing Seward as secretary of state, but also enabling Seward to oppose him in cabinet meetings and assist in the resolution of important crises throughout the Civil War.

Buchanan was left with broken dreams and disappointed hopes. He essentially remained neutral throughout the election, hoping that one of the other three candidates, including Lincoln, would win, maybe in a divided vote that would go to the House of Representatives.

Instead, it was much more of a flea than Buchanan had anticipated. Lincoln won eighteen states—every one of the non slave states' electoral votes, with the exception of three of the seven from New Jersey, for a total of 303. Kentucky, Tennessee, and Virginia were chosen as border states by Bell. Breckenridge won the rest of the South, which included eleven states and 72 electoral votes. Stephen Douglas, who had spent his entire political career building up to this race, received just a split vote from New Jersey and the state of Missouri, totaling only twelve electoral votes.

Buchanan would have to make numerous decisions in the four months between November 6, 1860, and March 4, 1861, because it was still the days of a considerable interim between the election and the next inauguration.
It would be the worst of times for the worst president.

On December 8, Howell Cobb resigned as Secretary of the Treasury, two days after a group of South Carolinians came to the White House to inform President Buchanan that their state was rapidly approaching secession. Cobb was his most trusted advisor, but he had reportedly struck an agreement with Attorney General Jeremiah Black that if Buchanan opposed secession, as he had informed South Carolinians, Cobb would leave. "The President and myself parted in the most friendly spirit," Cobb wrote to his wife. "We both see and feel the need, and we both regret that it must be so."

The shuffles then began, although to no apparent end. Cobb's position at the Treasury was filled by Philip F. Thomas of Maryland, the commissioner of patents. The secretary of state, Lewis Cass, resigned the next day because Buchanan refused to authorize soldiers to defend the Union forts in Charleston, particularly Fort Sumter. Buchanan was only somewhat saddened by Cass' departure since he thought Cass was incompetent. Even if his initiatives in locations like Paraguay and Juan de Fuca had been inept, the president was effectively operating the State Department himself. This promoted Jeremiah Black to state, and Edwin Stanton, a Republican who was in California on federal business, from Jeremiah Black's assistant to attorney general. That same day, another member of Buchanan's brain trust, Senator John Slidell of Louisiana, arrived at the White House, and when he left, it was the last time the two ever spoke.

Those three days in December devastated Buchanan and could not have been worse for those who still felt the Union might be saved. Georgia was gone if Cobb was gone. If Slidell refused to talk to Buchanan, Louisiana would be lost. Buchanan made another blunder when he authorized Mississippi Secretary of the Interior Jacob Thompson to travel to North Carolina to meet with secessionist representatives. Thompson had volunteered to resign before doing so, but Buchanan, evidently hoping to prevent the two states from seceding, let him depart.

The nation now believed Buchanan was a secessionist agent. On December 17, the most prominent newspaper editor in the North, Horace Greeley of the New York Tribune, published an editorial in which he declared, among other things, that the president was insane—perhaps not physically, but certainly symbolically in the face of catastrophe.

By December 20, the governor of South Carolina had dispatched a letter requesting that Buchanan immediately turn over Fort Sumter. "If South Carolina should attack any of these forts, she will then become the assailant in a war against the United States..." wrote Buchanan. This would be not merely a just cause of war, but also the start of hostilities." Knowing of Buchanan's likely response, the governor retracted his letter.

It was the closest Buchanan came to being forceful during his lame-duck period—or possibly even earlier. It was his last chance to save the Union, and perhaps if he had published the reply he never sent, it might have worked. Things were going fast, and someone needed to throw a big boulder in their way. Buchanan simply couldn't bring himself to do it.

When Cass left, he told everyone that Buchanan had panic attacks on a regular basis and spent most of his time praying or crying. On

December 20, Buchanan attended a wedding reception, reportedly in good health, but there was a ruckus midway through the reception. "Madam, do you suppose the house is on fire?" Buchanan questioned a female guest.

The right of property in slaves was recognized by granting free people distinct political rights, granting them the right to represent, and burdening them with direct taxes on three-fifths of their slaves; authorizing the importation of slaves for a period of twenty years; and stipulating for the rendition of fugitives from labor... They have encouraged and enabled thousands of our slaves to flee their homes, and those who have remained have been incited to servile insurgency through emissaries, literature, and photographs.

A geographical line has been established across the Union, and all of the states north of that line have banded together to elect a man to the high position of President of the United States whose ideas and goals are anti-slavery. He is to be entrusted with the administration of the Common Government since he has stated that "government cannot permanently endure half slave, half free" and that the public mind must believe that slavery is on its way out.

It was the same in the other states when they penned their reasons—make that one reason, singular—for leaving the Union. Mississippi's proclamation contained six sentences that chastised the North for luring slaves to flee and become free, despite the fact that almost no slaves from Mississippi made it to the North, needing to pass through several other slave states.

Whereas, the election of Abraham Lincoln and Hannibal Hamlin to the offices of president and vice-president of the United States of America, by a sectional party avowedly hostile to domestic institutions and to the peace and security of the people of the State of Alabama, was preceded by many and dangerous infractions of the constitution of the United S

Several old heads tried to think of solutions. Before leaving for his place in the Confederate legislature, ex-President John Tyler joyfully visited with Buchanan—Tyler's first time back in the White House in nearly two decades. Tyler was allowed to gather together anybody he wanted by the lame-duck president, but Buchanan could not necessarily accept anything Tyler proposed. The Compromise Committee of Thirteen, chaired by Kentucky's John Crittenden, only produced a solution that bent everything southward—allowing slavery and strengthening the Fugitive Slave Law, which no Northerner could ever accept.

Buchanan debated whether to reinforce Fort Sumter, hoping to fool South Carolina into firing the opening shot. Then he might be able to win a brief fight and reassemble the Humpty Dumpty nation.

Otherwise, he continued repeating a dictum that was as perplexing as it was ineffective. As a rigorous constitutional constructionist, Buchanan would argue that no state could secede because states waived their ability to do so by signing the original contract. On the other hand, he said that as president, he had no authority to bring them back into the Union, nor could he initiate a military strike to control the seceding states without congressional consent. Congress, which was becoming more Republican as Democrats from the South vacated their seats, would have been willing to do so, but Buchanan discouraged it. Militias were swiftly organizing throughout the South, and conscription was not yet in place in the North, thus each passing day made it more impossible to have a quick-ending combat in Charleston, or perhaps anyplace else.

Buchanan became despondent after having exhausted all possibilities for reconciliation before the March 4 deadline, when Lincoln would eventually take control. In his final weeks, he spent the most of his time composing letters and sipping Madeira. He would frequently invite a congressman or two or a cabinet official to stay in the White House, not for safety, but in the hope that something, anything, might happen to change the trajectory of his presidency.

In his four years, Buchanan had had few achievements. There were commercial ventures to Japan and China, for example, which helped to open up those markets. Despite the Pig War, the United States' northern border was stable. There were some technological advances—the first oil well was drilled, Elisha Otis invented a safe elevator, the transatlantic cable was laid, and the Pony Express began—but even these were hampered by the depression that followed the Panic of 1857, the abrupt end to a dozen years of plenty caused by Buchanan's support for the Dred Scott decision.

Buchanan conducted one more cabinet meeting the night before Lincoln's inauguration. Major Robert Anderson delivered an urgent communication to Buchanan the next morning, as he was preparing for the inauguration. After weeks of telling everyone that he was safe as commander of Fort Sumter, he now declared it would take 20,000 troops to secure the fort in the event of an attack, another blunder on Buchanan's part that would blow up a month later when the fort was attacked. He couldn't do anything else now.

Buchanan summoned his carriage and proceeded to Lincoln's hotel. He was claimed to have a cheerful look on the trip when he informed Lincoln, "My dear sir, if you are as happy in entering the White House as I shall feel on returning to Wheatland, you are a happy man indeed."

"Mr. President, I cannot say that I shall enter it with much pleasure, but I assure you that I shall do everything in my power to maintain the high standards set by my illustrious predecessors who have occupied it," Lincoln is supposed to have said.

Sharpshooters peeked from rooftops and platoons of soldiers lined the approach to the Capitol for what was thought to be the first time. As they approached the inaugural stand, the guy known as the Greatest. President. Ever., and certainly the Worst, saw an empty crane swinging from the dome, and lying in sorrowful repose nearby was Freedom, the great bronze figure it was to have carried.

When James Buchanan took office, there was no country more fascinating to other countries than the United States. Democracy in America, Alexis de Tocqueville's cross between a travelog and a political treatise, piqued the interest of Europeans who had previously considered the United States as an inconspicuous piece of territory too far away to worry about.

It took until the late 1840s for the adventure bug to draw European travelers to the expanding country over the Atlantic, and everyone seemed to have an opinion—some snobbish and critical, others wide-eyed and praising—on what America was and what Americans were.

Despite, or perhaps because of, its numerous annoyances, the United States enjoyed an almost continuous economic boom for a decade or more before Buchanan assumed office in March 1857. New cities sprouted up not just in the expanding West, but also in the East— "one flourishing town after another," noted the scientist and explorer Charles Lyell of his journey across upstate New York. "Utica," "Syracuse," and "Auburn." There were no beggars or shoeless persons unless they chose to be. "Everywhere, the most unequivocal proof of prosperity and rapid progress in agriculture, commerce, and great public works."

It had only been eighty years since the signing of the Declaration of Independence and a dozen years since George Washington first filled this unusual office of "president," unknown in the civilized world. In other countries, no one could be king, but it appeared that anyone could be the guy who controlled the United States, as fourteen before Buchanan had been.

As a result, it appeared to European visitors that there had emerged some human features that were unquestionably American. And Americanism, if such a thing existed, had been born. "Whether they arrived in New York, Philadelphia, or Boston, foreign visitors were struck by the bustle, enterprise, and rough-and-ready cheerfulness of the people." "Men talked about money and had it," Allan Nevins wrote in his fundamental study of the time, "Ordeal of the Union.

Almost anything appeared permissible, almost anything seemed feasible. It was regularly seen that the analyst who was horrified by some major flaw could find a compensatory grace registered with equal vigor. America had an alarming sum of violence, but it also possessed the world's most active nonviolent movement. It was cursed by rampant intemperance in its major towns and throughout its frontiers, although vast territories outlawed booze with inexorable zeal. It appeared to be the most licentious of lands in some areas, and the most puritanically strait-laced in others. Americans were open about being materialistic and hooked to money, but they were also the most idealistic and generous people on the planet. The country saw appalling displays of religious intolerance at times, but it took pleasure in the general tolerance of its laws and traditions. The entire range of human faults and achievements appeared to be depicted with greater emphasis and color than in previous nations.

Chapter 6:
The Legacy of the Least of the Lesser Presiden

It was a snowy midwinter Saturday morning in Washington, DC, when I parked the car along Sixteenth Street, the White House in the distance a little less than a mile distant. Meridian Hill Park, which had been a mansion estate tract for over a century, was located on the east side of the street for a few blocks.

A young couple and their female acquaintance were the only other persons in the park. Every now and then, they'd pull off to a lovely area, and the friend would photograph the newlyweds kissing, most likely for a preview wedding album.

I was there for a different reason, but they seemed to have a plan. I inquired about the location of the Buchanan statue. They simply shrugged. "Is Buchanan the president?" inquired the young man. "Don't you think it's unlikely here?"

But there it was, descending from a rise in the park's southeast corner. A long curve of granite with an eight-foot-high bronze statue of Buchanan sitting in repose on a pedestal at its center. A stone statue of a mythical male Justice stands at one end of the curve, while a female Diplomacy stands at the other, both naked to the waist. On a side panel, an old friend, Jeremiah Black, refers to him as "the incorruptible statesman whose walk was upon the mountain ranges of the law."

When I arrived at the monument, the snow seemed to be weighing a little on Buchanan's shoulders, as if he knew I was coming, like Brutus for Caesar, come to bury, not praise.

Harriet Lane Johnston, Buchanan's cherished niece, left a bequest in her will to create two monuments to her uncle, one in Stony Batter, where he was born, and the other in Washington. She died in 1903, leaving the funds to the Commonwealth of Pennsylvania for the one in Stony Batter and to Congress for the one in Washington. The request provided for the commissioning of the monuments every fifteen years. A friend, famed Washington banker Lawrason Riggs, purchased the land in Stony Batter and took over management of the monument—a thirty-one-foot-high pyramid composed of fifty tons of native stones and mortar. Riggs arranged for 35 workers to construct the pyramid and developed a tiny railroad to transport the stone from a neighboring mountain to the location. The Pennsylvania General Assembly oversaw the entire project, and the eighteen-and-a-half-acre Buchanan Birthplace State Park opened in 1911.

It was not simple in Washington, as nothing ever is. When Johnston's donation was revealed, there were presidential outdoor memorials. The first was a statue of Andrew Jackson on horseback in Lafayette Square, across from the White House, begun in 1847, and the Washington Memorial's cornerstone was laid the following year, but the obelisk was not finished until 1885, its construction suspended for more than two decades due to a lack of funds. In 1867, two years after Lincoln's assassination, the city of Washington erected a statue of him at City Hall. The Army of the Tennessee finally secured enough funds in 1902 to begin work on a statue of Ulysses S. Grant on horseback near the Capitol, but it took sculptor Henry Merwin Shrady nearly twenty years to finish.

These four were either great military heroes or martyrs, almost secondary presidents, and even then, people were hesitant to fund such enterprises. Though Johnston's legacy would cover at least the cost of the Buchanan memorial, congressmen were hesitant to celebrate an obscure and, frankly, disliked and unremembered president thirty-five years after his death.

As time passed, multiple measures were submitted in Congress to create a grander memorial to Lincoln, three of which failed until President William Howard Taft pushed through a $300,000 grant in 1910.

The Johnston grant had long since been forgotten. With the money's fifteen-year limit nearing, someone uncovered the grant proposal, and the commission was approved a few weeks before it expired, in the spring of 1918. Even so, it took until 1930 to find a site, an architect, and a sculptor to complete the project, beating even the next celebrated monumental president, Thomas Jefferson, who received his rotunda thirteen years later.

While he had a strong supporter in his niece, who was far more popular than her Uncle Nunc both during and after his presidency, Buchanan was never popular again, even after he left office.

"Frankly, he was just vilified," recalled Patrick Clarke, director of Wheatland, Buchanan's Lancaster estate. "It wasn't just historians who were harsh on Buchanan. When he initially returned to Lancaster, the animosity was palpable. It was especially powerful in 1863, when the Battle of Gettysburg took place just a few miles away."

Clarke recounted the early days in Lancaster of John F. Reynolds, the son of Buchanan's best friend, also named John Reynolds. When Buchanan was in the United States Senate in 1837, he recommended his son to West Point, where he began a remarkable and spectacular military career. When the Civil War began, he was promoted to brigadier general and deployed to the Army of the Potomac, the major battle formation. Reynolds was arrested once by the Confederate army, but he was exchanged for another prisoner thanks to a Confederate military acquaintance he had served with before the war. Soon after the devastating battle of Fredericksburg, Virginia, in the spring of 1863, Lincoln was looking for a replacement for Joseph Hooker as his military commander and met Reynolds, who turned down the job because Lincoln indicated he couldn't protect him from politicians who might oppose. Instead, another Pennsylvanian, George Meade, took control.

Reynolds, however, was shot in the back of the neck and killed on the first day of the fight at Gettysburg. There are now three memorials to Reynolds at Gettysburg and another on the apron of Philadelphia's City Hall, but there was a less fortunate aftermath in Wheatland.

"The entire family blamed Buchanan for his death," Wheatland's Clarke explained. Ellie Reynolds had been like a sister to Buchanan's niece Harriet Lane, and the younger John was as adored by Buchanan as his own nephews.

"The father, John Reynolds, was no longer alive, but the family blamed Buchanan for the Civil War." Their most favored son had vanished. The father was so close to Buchanan that he was the first person to sign his petition to become a Mason, which is a huge deal. After that, all of General Reynolds' siblings turned against Buchanan."

The prologue to Philip Klein's sympathetic biography has Buchanan contemplating his fate at his home in Wheatland a few days before the Battle of Gettysburg. It was probably fabricated, but it told the tense story of how people thought of Buchanan at the time.

Occasionally, small groups of horsemen would ride out of town, bound towards the Susquehanna River, ten miles to the west. Most of the riders seemed to be going about their business, but as the pike passed through the expansive grounds of Wheatland, former President Buchanan's residence, some would yell, "You damned rebel!" or "I hope they burn you out like they did Thad Stevens!"

Buchanan had walked down from his house to his favorite evening spot, the spring on the lower lawn along the pike. He enjoyed peering over the low stone parapet into the clear water and seeing the moss and white sand gently whirling in the undercurrent. He'd never found the sunsets more calming or the world more serene than here, under the willow beside his Wheatland spring. But not this evening. Wheatland would be standing or in ruins tomorrow. Was he living, dead, or a foolish souvenir of this terrible, unimaginable war? He didn't know, and he didn't care much...

Buchanan went straight to the study after entering the house and began writing. If the rebels arrived, they'd find him hard at work, writing his account about Mr. Buchanan's Administration on the Eve of Rebellion.

Buchanan would not die or be taken; he would live on when the fight was over. He worked on his presidential memoirs but did not publish them until after the Civil War ended, despite the fact that the majority of the book was completed by 1862. He felt honor bound not to bother his successor, Lincoln, with his sentiments while fighting a war. While Buchanan despised the war, he supported Lincoln throughout it, expecting that it would conclude with the Union revived.

He wrote the book in the third person, as the title suggests. It's dull, but it's packed with information. Buchanan relied heavily on official sources and information gleaned and saved from friends' and officials' correspondence to him. He commanded some of those people to send him copies of anything they possessed, but many of them did not want to be bothered—after all, there was a war going on.

Former politicians of all stripes, but especially ex-presidents, have been expected to produce memoirs in recent decades, but prior to Buchanan, only Thomas Jefferson had any significant success with autobiography, writing one at the age of seventy-seven in 1821. In truth, most presidents did not live long enough after their public service to do so.

Buchanan's book is important for only one reason: he blamed the Northern anti-slavery movement for the Civil War and its escalation during his presidency. It was hardly an uncharted territory, because it was shared by both moderate and fire-breathing Democrats. The North had accepted at least Southern slavery for so long that many people assumed it would always be that way. When it became evident, however, that with all of the westward expansion, the South would soon convert from an equal part to a minority one, abolitionists, who had previously been a nuisance, began really troubling Southerners. According to Buchanan, the agitators from the North were principally to blame for the growing split, which eventually became intractable.

This interpretation appears inane in modern Civil War histories. Slavery existed in the South, and the South desired to keep it that way. The slaveholders' fixation, combined with the pride the majority of the South felt in its traditions, split the Union. Even though most anti-slavery advocates in the North wanted the institution abolished, they did not want to abolish the South, but rather transform it. It was similar to a partner who wishes to change the other's habits rather than divorce. The concept of secession was entirely Southern. It was Southern to hold on to an immoral and, finally, untenable institution. Even though the increasingly loud anti-slavery voice irritated them, it was Southerners who wanted to leave and fight over it if necessary.

Buchanan had hoped to have someone else write the book, and had first asked his former attorney general and secretary of state, Jeremiah Black, to do so for a considerable sum of money, $7,000. Black, on the other hand, quickly discovered that he disagreed with Buchanan's appraisal of so many aspects, particularly because Buchanan wanted to declare that he was completely behind Lincoln after the war began. "I am eager to vindicate the previous administration," Black wrote to his former employer, "but I cannot do so on the ground you now occupy." So Buchanan decided to go it alone.

Buchanan was the voice of the Northerners-started-it strain of Civil War interpretation to the extent that his memoirs were regarded seriously and became part of the political air following the war. His reputation, or what remained of it, was shattered even further after the war, for even those who blamed Lincoln principally for it never absolved Buchanan—and at least Lincoln was able to restore the Union in the end.

After the war, Buchanan still wanted someone to write his official biography, and he hired two separate Philadelphians, James Shunk and William Reed, to do it at various periods. Shunk and his wife spent a year in Wheatland, taking notes from discussions with the previous president, but they never finished their book. Reed, a Philadelphia publisher, took over after that, but he procrastinated and never sought the Shunks' notes.

Long after Buchanan died, the Johnstons—his niece, Harriet, and her husband—began looking for writers. They eventually decided on George Ticknor Curtis, a barrister who had written a few historical books. Ironically, he was Dred Scott's defense lawyer in the Supreme Court case, although correspondence back and forth regarding the book negotiations in the Library of Congress collection never addresses this. The two-volume Life of James Buchanan, published in 1883, fifteen years after the subject's death, is a jumble of irrelevant or obscure correspondence. Curtis must have felt obligated to incorporate everything the Johnstons had given him because they were his patrons. It appears that it was written by a lawyer, not a stylist or even a creative author. The next biography, by Philip Klein, would not be published until 1962. Klein's writing is fluent, yet he does not provide a compelling story. He was a historian, and like Curtis, he appears to want to include every little detail to demonstrate his meticulousness. It is an apologia, and after reading it's more than 500 pages, a reader who does not know American history would assume Buchanan was high on the presidential mountains of Washington and Jefferson, not in the valley with Pierce and Harding.

Jean H. Baker's biography for the American Presidents series, written in 2004, is brief and, if not David McCulloughesque, certainly readable. It comes to reason, however, that it would never have been allocated unless it was absolutely necessary; after all, Buchanan was one of the presidents and had to be included in the series.

The Corcoran Gallery in Washington, DC, closed in 2014, and its 17,000 items were relocated in 2015. More than 6,500 of them went to the National Gallery of Art, the museum's sibling in Washington, DC. The National Gallery did, however, reject a portrait of Buchanan by George Peter Alexander Healy. It could have been an error, but it was an insult. The will of his niece, Harriet Lane Johnston, founded the entire concept of the Smithsonian's broad collection becoming a "National Gallery of Art." Her personal art collection, which included a favorite piece, the Healy portrait, was included in Johnston's bequest.

It is safe to assume that, if not for his niece's diligence and her long life and social importance in Washington, as well as Philip Klein's infatuation with a reasonably renowned man in his hometown, Buchanan would have left no legacy at all. The postal agency published a presidential series of stamps with a bust of Buchanan facing right on a drab gray background in 1938. It was a fifteen-cent stamp for the fifteenth president, although it was probably rarely used because no postal fee was fifteen cents or any multiple of it throughout its period in circulation. There was also a brief series of presidential twenty-two cent stamps issued in 1986, featuring every president up to that point, but few of these saw actual circulation.

However, considering Buchanan's presidency is not a pointless exercise. My wife received a fellowship at Stanford University in the late 1990s, where one of Buchanan's opponents for an unassailable presidency, Herbert Hoover, was an alumnus. It was the height of the first Silicon Valley tech boom, and one of the guiding principles was that failure was a positive thing. If an entrepreneur had not failed, he would not have sought to "push the envelope," as another popular phrase at the time went. There was no successful Silicon Valley icon who had not failed, not Hewlett-Packard, not Steve Wozniak, and certainly not Steve Jobs.

So perhaps viewing Buchanan's sequence of failures as a worthy study of how to become a better president is a positive thing. And presidents who want to be the standard-bearer for a political party should take note. The Democratic Party was severely weakened, if not completely dissolved, as a result of Buchanan's administration. Prior to Buchanan, Democrats had elected ten of the fifteen presidents, with several winning by huge percentages. In the Electoral College, for example, James Monroe received all but one vote. In the 1860s election, the party broke into three sections, ensuring Lincoln's victory. Worse, there was only one Democratic president in the next half-century—Grover Cleveland. The schism in the party caused by Buchanan was seismic. Republicans succeeded Republicans even after bad presidencies like Andrew Johnson's and Ulysses S. Grant's. There has never been such a presidential legacy.

Much of Buchanan's failure appears to stem from his obtuseness and clinging to some vague idea of what he thought a strict reading of the Constitution was, which meant that the president was mostly an administrator and that Congress and the states should dictate the country's direction. To be sure, he broke from it whenever he pleased, most notably in his influence on the Dred Scott case.

Still, given the contrarian mindset in which I frequently find myself, it might not be a terrible idea for the next presidents to scrutinize not only Washington or Lincoln, but also Buchanan, before taking office. Most presidents will never have the opportunity to be those two men we usually remember on Presidents' Day in February. Those possible presidents are most likely from ordinary or upper-middle-class backgrounds, have received good educations, and have been involved in partisan politics at some point. That's more like Buchanan than Washington or Lincoln. Chances are, they've developed intractable opponents, or enemies who are so preoccupied with them that they can't get them out of their heads, as Buchanan did with Stephen Douglas. They've very likely formed friends with doctrinal people, much like Buchanan did with his Southern pals. They have most likely served in positions they afterwards felt were minor, like Buchanan did in Russia, and may have pulled off an upset in policy or an election, as Buchanan did in the Russian ministry.

If those people can learn from someone who has risen to their level, Buchanan could be the man. It would be difficult to aspire to a middle-of-the-road presidency like Calvin Coolidge or James Monroe. What egotist, such as a possible president, wants to end up in the middle? It's natural to wish that a future phrase wouldn't be like Buchanan's.

When Buchanan died, he was the last living member of the session of the United States House of Representatives that began in December 1821, halfway through James Monroe's term. He died just before U. S. Grant was elected. As a result, his public life spanned many of the nation's ups and downs. He spent his latter years like any senior who was the head of a family would: he scrutinized every relative's and friend's finances down to the cent. He distributed hidden sums of money to persons in need. He spent a lot of time walking around his garden. He traveled a little, usually to see old acquaintances in Philadelphia, or to Baltimore to see his niece, or to Bedford Springs, where he had taken the waters for years. He even went to the Jersey Shore—and had a Jersey Shore-type experience, being afflicted by gout and unable to drink his favorite, Madeira, for the whole of his agonizing stay.

Despite the fact that a large crowd, possibly several thousand people, attended his funeral in Lancaster, no one made a meaningful speech. According to one speaker quoted in the Lancaster Intelligencer, "Starting at Stony Batter, a barefoot boy climbed to the highest office in the world." The identical procedure was done by an Illinois rail-splitter. The impact of such an example is immeasurable. A republic is the only place on the planet where this is conceivable."

A sigh. A cynical raising of the eyebrow. A tired ode to the Worst. President. Ever.

Printed in Great Britain
by Amazon

39370527R00050